Practical Tips and Advice for Making a Simple Budget

Stop Living from Paycheck to Paycheck!

Practical Tips and Advice for Making a Simple Budget

Stop Living from Paycheck to Paycheck!

Gerard Hoffman

Your Free Gift

As a way of saying thank you for your purchase,

a free Simple Budget spreadsheet is available

to readers of this book.

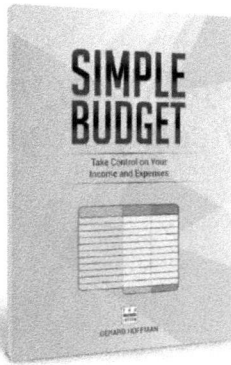

Enter the link below to your browser

to get free instant access.

https://mailchi.mp/3724c74e2d97/your-free-gift

Contents

Introduction

*"A budget is telling your money WHERE
to go instead of wondering where it WENT"
Dave Ramsey*

When you think of financial advice, the term
'budget' is typically one of the words that spring to mind.
It's no wonder, because people are talking about it all the
time! For most people, however, this word has a lot of
negative connotations and emotions associated with it.
*Stop eating out with friends. Stop spending on little luxuries that
you want. Stop traveling so frequently. Stop buying that cup of
coffee.* Basically, a budget feels like an indirect way of
telling you to stop having fun. All of a sudden, it feels like
you can't spend money on the things that made you
happy, like you used to every time payday came around.

Budgeting feels restrictive, like a barrier to having fun. Naturally, if it feels restrictive and unpleasant, right now, you're probably still asking yourself if this is a good idea. Do you want the truth?

The answer is *yes,* this *is* a good idea, and *yes,* you do need a budget. You see, building the wealth of tomorrow starts from the actions that you take *today.* We're here to take a different approach and to start thinking about budgeting as less restrictive and more as a way of creating awareness. It is about being aware of what you are *actually* spending on and then cutting back on the areas that you *don't* need to be spending.

In doing so, you're creating room to spend money on the things you genuinely want. From a financial perspective, a budget is defined as a set amount of money, that is assigned to be spent on a specific resource or activity. A budget is necessary for a healthy financial life because there's a darker, more sinister that should worry you. A word that can lead to *much worse* than what a budget could ever do. The dreaded four-letter word that no one wants to be shackled to, weighing you down and keeping you from your dreams. *Debt.* Oh yes, debt can be a nasty burden, and if you thought budgeting was crippling your freedom, wait until you're in debt, and you suddenly realize retirement is fast approaching.

You *do not want* to be tied down to debt and spend the next several years of your life paying it off while you continue to live paycheck to paycheck as your goals and dreams slip further and further away from you. A Pew Research study pointed out an interesting fact, which was that more than half of Americans tend to spend more than what they're earning each month – so it comes as no surprise just how quickly debt can be accumulated. As of 2017, Experian, a consumer and business credit reporting website, revealed how the average American has $6,354 in just credit card debt alone, and upwards of $24,700 in other non-mortgage debt. Could you imagine having to deal with this once you retire with no source of steady income coming in from your 9-5 job anymore? That is more alarming than the idea of having a budget, wouldn't you agree? Some people manage to successfully get themselves out of debt while others struggle for years with little to no progress. The ones that succeed did so because they had a plan, and that plan was...*having a budget.* It wasn't a magic formula, it wasn't inheritance, and it wasn't because they 'got lucky' and had a windfall. They worked hard, sacrificed, and cut-back for the more significant long-term goal.

Many people wonder which of their expenses costs them the most and how they can spend their money differently to save more effectively. In this book, I will show you where your money goes and how to find out what you spend the most money on. You will also start planning your expenses better. For several years I had financial problems that I could not cope with. My situation started to get worse. To solve it, I decided to take out a loan. Looking back, this wasn't a great decision. Eventually, I had to take out another loan, which caused me to fall into a credit spiral. I didn't want to live like that. So I chose to analyze my expenses and drew some conclusions.

I realized that my life would only become more complicated if I didn't change the way I thought about money. Thankfully, after a lot of thinking and hard work, I was able to get out of this situation successfully. Since then, I've been committed to advising and helping other people to regain financial freedom. I would like to share my experience with you and to show you the way out of financial problems. Using the methods of budget management described in this book, you will understand what is happening with your money, what products and services you can save money on, and what costs you can get rid of once and for all.

I have often heard people say things such as "I earn money, but I feel like I never have any money," "I don't know where and when I even spend money?" Your frustration builds up over time, and you don't feel good about it. You start to worry about your future. One thing to keep in mind is the importance of facing these problems without delay. The ways to reduce expenses and stick to your budget described in this book will allow you to change your life immediately. Each of the chapters in this book will guide you, in detail, through different types of expenses and offer advice on how to deal with them. Thanks to the suggestions provided in this book, you'll finally be able to start your financial journey toward spending less.

People thank me for helping them change their lives. In this book, I have included the *exact* same advice that I have given to those same people. With my help and experience, you will be able to spend less money. In managing your budget, you will start to feel more prepared for the unexpected expenses life throws at us all.

Chapter 1:
How Will Having
a Budget Help Me?

"If you fail to plan, then you plan to fail"
Benjamin Franklin

Think about this saying for a minute. It rings pretty true when it comes to your finances. If you don't have a plan about *how* you're going to be spending your own money to meet your needs and wants, you end up being overwhelmed. In fact, 30% of Americans are stressed about their finances. Simply ask yourself for a moment: *How well are you managing your finances?* Be honest with yourself. Are you saving diligently and accumulating a nice little bank balance consistently every month? Are you unable to save because you feel like you're living paycheck to paycheck? Or are you not saving at all because you're not really giving it much thought, or you're relying on your family or your spouse whenever an emergency pops up? If your answer *isn't* the first one, you're living unsustainably and irresponsibly.

Managing your money seems easy enough, but sometimes you can lose track of it. Most people have no idea where their money is going, and before the next paycheck rolls around, they are scratching their heads in confusion, wondering where their *last* paycheck went. How could it have finished so quickly? When it feels like you 'hardly spent anything' at all.

Budgets Explained

Budgeting. It's a fancy term for keeping track of your expenses and where your hard-earned money is going. What does your money get spent on? How much of it goes out, and how much is left over after all the bills have been paid? Ideally, you would want to spend a lot less than what you're earning, thereby saving, investing, or putting the rest aside for a rainy day. Constantly scraping the bottom of the bank to make ends meet is a sure sign that it's time to change and do something about it.

Most people are terrified of the "B" word, but with careful planning, a budget could turn out to be your best friend. A successful business doesn't operate without a budget, so why are we doing the same thing with our personal finances? Especially when it is the key to financial freedom.

Essentially, a budget is a plan for how your income is going to be used, whether it goes towards rent payments, mortgage payments, car payments, groceries, medical bills, miscellaneous expenses, savings for a vacation. Some of these are *needs,* and some of these are *wants*, but the one thing both categories have in common is that they *cost money.*

There are many different types of budgets that you could follow. You could choose to follow a budget that someone has meticulously planned, detailed, or written about in a book or published online. You could download several budget templates, or you could go ahead and create your own budget that is specifically tailored to your life and your needs. Budgets can last for a short period like a few days, weeks, or months, but they could also last for a more extended period, like a few years. Some people even follow the same budget for *decades.* A budget is a *PLAN*, a strategic, specific, and purposeful plan that you follow with your money so that your money can go *as far as it can* using a budget.

Why Is Budgeting So Important?

Without a budget, you're missing out on opportunities to *build* on your savings. A budget helps you spend wisely *and* identify opportunities, as well as ways to keep more money in your pocket, by modifying the way you spend. It could teach you tricks to cleverly manage your money that you didn't learn at school, like saving *first* and paying your bills second. It keeps you accountable for your spending and helps keep away the stress of living beyond your means.

With a budget, you're also put in touch with the reality of your financial situation. The areas where you need to tighten your purse strings are pointed out to you, in addition to in which categories you can afford to relax. With a budget, every cent is accounted for; you're never wondering where it all went or how it could have vanished so quickly.

Most people are put off by the very thought of having a budget because they associate it with restrictions and hassle. They believe they earn too little to budget or want to enjoy life more than they want to restrict their spending. They fail to realize that the secret to financial independence *is* through a budget. What you need are reasons concrete enough to change your mind and shift your perspective about what it means to live on a budget. The better you become at sticking to it, the easier it is to make your money go further. A budget is vital for developing a robust, financial game-plan, and these are the reasons why:

- **It Keeps You Focused** - A proper budget will help you stay focused on what you want. When you sit down to create it, you need to ask yourself what your life goals are and how your finances fit into those goals. Asking this question forces you to keep your budget simple. Every part of your budget will have a specific purpose in the overall grand scheme of your life. For example, if your goal is to provide for and comfortably support a family one day, you need to start getting into the *mindset* of providing for a family, and this begins *before* you get married.

- **It Stops the Guessing Game** - Rather than *guessing* where your money went and what you spent it on, you know *exactly* how much money you're making and how effectively you're allocating it to cover your basic needs while still saving your income. The transparency of your budget could lead to a better understanding of your spending habits, and you can communicate this to your family or significant other if you needed to.

- **It Stops You From *Over*spending -** If you've got a bad habit of overspending, this is where a budget comes in really handy. For example, let's say you have a designated amount allocated for a category like *Health and Fitness,* and you've assigned $100 a month to this category. You spend $75 on your gym membership and $25 on health supplements; then, you know that membership for the new yoga studio that opened up down the street will have to wait until next month. Or, you could use this as a reference point that you might need to re-shift your priorities and how you're spending that money. Overspending is a big issue for many people that leads to a lot of financial stress.

- **It Encourages You to Think About Priorities -** Learning how to focus on only the things which *matter to you* is going to be the focus of your spending habits if you have a budget. When you have a specific goal to focus on, it can be easier to determine what you want to buy and what you don't. Goals help you redirect your resources to where it matters most, which is precisely the purpose of a budget. If you know your priority is to save for a vacation with your family, you're not going to want to spend on getting a new t-shirt which you don't need, even if it is on sale. If you know your priority is to take your parents out to a nice dinner for their anniversary, you're going to redirect your resources towards that *instead* of buying another pair of shoes you don't need.

- **It Ensures You Don't Spend Money You Don't Have** - Without a budget, you're going to spend more than what you earn each month. Doing this will significantly limit your future spending power since the income you make in the future is already going to be directed toward paying off your debt. If you think budgeting restricts your spending, think about what it would feel like to see a significant portion of your salary going towards loan repayment. All those long hours you spent working to earn a living, and yet having hardly anything to show for it at the end of the day. Imagine the stress of not having enough to pay for necessities like food, rent, your mortgage, bills, school fees, and more when most of your income is already committed to repaying your debt. A budget is exactly the thing you need to save you from such a predicament.

- **It Helps You Reach Your Goal** - A budget is a plan. That plan is to help you prioritize your spending. With a budget, you can allocate your money towards *more important* goals. *Life-changing goals.* Imagine if your goal were to pay off your debt. When you start seeing just how quickly your debt can be reduced – as you pay it off with the money you've now saved from cutting down on unnecessary purchases – you'll be motivated to keep towards the finish line of becoming debt-free. Your financial goals draw one step closer with each payment that you make. Getting rid of debt is one of the most liberating financial experiences, because, without that burden, more doors and possibilities start to open. You could start your own business. Save for the dream home you've wanted for so long. Take that vacation with your family you've been wanting. Pursue your passion with the funds you now have to spare. Your budget *is* the plan that helps you accumulate money for such goals and allows you to track your progress to ensure that you're on course to reach them.

- **It Helps You Save Money -** Without a budget, you will be saving less than what you *could be saving*. That's because, with a budget, you assign your money to do certain things already like saving more money, for example. By making *savings* a budget item, and automatically putting money into a savings account, you're beginning to build wealth. It's actually hard to resist the urge to save *more* as the numbers in your bank account begin to climb. All that money which was previously spent on buying frivolous and unnecessary items is now channeled and put to good use by saving it instead. Increasing your savings, and putting more money aside than you were before, will leave you with enough to put some of it aside to pay off any existing debts, or save for a rainy day. Less shopping, more savings and debt-paying, and you're one step closer to financial freedom without the burden of debt weighing you down.

- **It Stops You From Worrying** - Without financial security, it's all too easy to default to always being worried about the future and what it will bring. That's where a budget comes in handy. It helps you *do* something about improving that future. *What if I lose my job one day? What if a major expense pops up? What if my business fails? What will happen when I retire? What do I do? What if there is an emergency that my life or the life of someone I love depends on?* Everyone should have an emergency fund just in case. These funds should be easily accessible and only to be used in the case of an *absolute emergency* when you have exhausted all other options. When you know you're collecting a nice little nest egg, you become a lot more confident about the future, since you no longer depend on anyone to get you through.

- **It Helps You Be More Flexible** - The beauty of a budget is that it is never rigid. You get to customize it, personalize it, and utilize it in the way that works best *for you*. You can move money around to cover specific categories, allowing you to recognize changing circumstances and *adjust* your finances accordingly. For example, if you have an unexpected increase in expenditure in one category, it can be covered by reducing the spending allocated to other categories to help balance it out. Let's say your electricity bill was unexpectedly expensive this month. You can compensate by downsizing your entertainment for the month.

- **It Encourages You to Remain Committed and Disciplined -** When you set a goal, commit to yourself that you *are* going to see it through to the end. That's really what a budget is – making a promise to yourself, a commitment that you're going to get your finances in order. Every action that you take, even the small ones, should bring you one step closer to your goal. Every day brings you that little bit further, so never allow yourself to get discouraged by the financial setbacks you encounter. Having a balanced budget shows that you are managing your finances with discipline and control. If you can exercise this kind of self-discipline when it comes to your finances, you can do it for the many other areas of your life where discipline was lacking before. It's hard to overstate the dramatic difference it will make to your life if you accomplish every goal you ever set for yourself because *you made a commitment* to stick to it. Setting a budget is the first steppingstone that could eventually lead to much greater things.

The fear that most people hold about how restrictive a budget can be is unfounded. *You* get to decide how much you want to spend on each category. If you want to put more money in your leisure activities fund, you can! As long as you *are* saving and meeting your other needs, you don't have to feel bad or guilty about it. However, once you set limits for yourself, you *need* to stick to them. If you're not doing this, then you may need to address that weakness.

Consequences of a Budget-Free Life

Living a budget-free life is like living a life without financial discipline. You *will* overspend because nothing is holding you back. No sense of purpose, no reason why you should hold onto your cash for a rainy day, no sense of responsibility. Nothing in life is ever certain, especially not our finances, and living without a budget is like living without a safety net. When you fall, you're going to fall hard.

Without a budget, you're going to be spending beyond your means; in the worst-case scenario, you're spending money *that's not yours to spend*. The latter is precisely how you end up knee-deep in debt. The disappointment, shock, frustration, anger, shame, and guilt that you feel over how you allowed yourself to reach this point is going to overwhelm you. Without a budget, you're always going to end up being caught off-guard by how much you've spent. A budget will always ensure that you are the one who remains in control of your spending. No longer do you have to wonder where your money went, because a budget is going to put you right back in the driver's seat.

The importance of being financially independent cannot be stressed enough. In times of emergencies, you can only ever truly depend on yourself. Relying on someone else for your finances will put you in a difficult position, especially if and when they are unable to help you out in that time of need. Single, married, young, old, or in a relationship, *everyone* should build a solid financial foundation to their name. You have the power within your hands not just to build and preserve our wealth for yourself, but for your families, especially if you choose to have kids. Financial planning may not be everyone's cup of tea, but it is a necessity if you ever hope to achieve the financial independence you want. Once you get started, you'll be even more driven to keep going. You'll realize just how empowering it can be not to have to rely on anyone for money, to be able to make your own decisions and to take pride in knowing you're able to take care of yourself should an unfortunate disaster strike.

A budget is not about limiting your fun. It's about taking *control* of your spending, opening doors to new opportunities by having extra money to move around. In fact, a budget could even lead to *more fun* if you plan wisely.

Financial Freedom Is Empowering

"It is not the man who has too little,
but the man who craves more, that is poor"
Seneca

Financial freedom can be incredibly empowering, and a budget is the *greatest and easiest* tool at your disposal right now to change your financial future. The moment you achieve financial freedom is the moment your life takes on a pivotal change for the better. Financial independence gives you the power you want and need to make changes in your life because it means that you no longer have to depend on anyone for your survival. That feeling is both powerful and liberating. You know that, regardless of what comes your way, you are now capable of ensuring your survival without relying on someone else to bail you out. Financial freedom gives you all the power to live your life on your own terms, the way you want it. You don't need to ask for permission from your spouse or your parents, perhaps even friends, or relatives, in the way you might have if you were relying on them for your finances.

Financial freedom means the power to make your own decisions and make the choices that are best for you. You *can* make your own rules when your life doesn't revolve around somebody else, which is quite possibly one of the best feelings being financially free rewards you with. The knowledge that you can take care of not just yourself, but your family, is a powerful feeling – one that gives you peace of mind because you now know that when it comes to your family's finances, you don't have to worry as much and have a safety net in place.

It's a powerful feeling, knowing that no matter what happens to you tomorrow, you will be okay regardless because you are financially free. If you were to lose your job tomorrow, that's okay because you've made the necessary financial preparations to take care of yourself until you get another job. If your car needed a fix tomorrow, that's okay because you've prepared for emergencies. No sense of helplessness, despair, or desperation will weigh on your mind, because when you're financially free, you know you're going to be okay. Don't take a back seat anymore when it comes to financial dominance, instead take charge, take control of your financial future. Why? Because *you can* do it.

Chapter 2:
Deciding What
Your Priorities Are

Before you begin, here's a thought that now needs to become permanently etched in your mind: *Budgeting is NOT about restrictions. It's about creating GREATER FREEDOM in your life.* Budgets are not the most fun activity in the world, but they're a crucial step to taking control of your finances. How many times have you found yourself at the end of the month, left wondering where your money went, and how it ran out so quickly? That's because you don't realize that it's the little things, and those small expenses, the ones we don't even give a second thought to, that add up. Without a proper budget to keep us in check, it becomes easier to spend your cash mindlessly without even thinking it through. Budgeting is about creating extra room in your finances so you can begin making smarter decisions with your money.

It seems awfully shallow to care so much about money, but that's the reality of it. Whether we like it or not, we need the money, and without it, we wouldn't be able to survive. It's a harsh truth we should learn to accept, even though we don't want to be that shallow. We need money to exist in this world, and many of us worry that we may not have enough money as we should or could. Money worries generally span from not having enough money to pay the bills for the month, financial security for the future, not having enough money for an emergency, and worries about not having enough to live on comfortably once you hit retirement. Financial security can be a significant cause of anxiety and stress for many, especially when we're not all rolling in millions and billions. Financial worries can take their toll on your mental health and cause serious anxiety and depression if they become chronic.

Better control. Less stress. Greater confidence. Better savings habits. More money tucked away for a rainy day and retirement day. More money to spend on things you want without compromising on your savings, breaking the bank, or scraping the bottom of the barrel. That is what a budget can do for your financial life. The only way to gain control of your finances once again is to start diligently tracking all your expenses each month to see exactly where your money is going. Keep track of it, even if you're spending a dollar on a candy bar. At the end of the month, take a good hard look at your spending patterns. You'll be able to see where unnecessary spending is taking place and where you need to cut back.

Understandably, budgeting for the very first time can be very stressful. Where do you start? What do you do? When do you do it? Take a deep breath. It's not going to be as bad as you think. That's why you're here right now, reading this very book – because you know that you want to do something about your budget, and you're looking for a straightforward way to do it correctly, so you're making as few mistakes as possible along the way.

Contrary to what most people think, you don't need to wait until you start making *more money* before you can begin budgeting. Budgeting should start *right now* because if you don't know where your money is going, you're going to find yourself just as broke even when you start making more money than you were before. Would you drive somewhere out of state without a map or navigation assistance of some sort? Probably not, unless you were feeling adventurous. You could head out in the general direction of your destination, but you'd find yourself lost along the way several times, and having to stop and ask for directions. It works the same way with your money.

A budget *tells your money where to go* every month. It is like a financial road map that helps you get from Point A to B in the most efficient way possible. When it comes to worries about money, just about everyone else in this world is in the same boat you are. Just about the only people who are probably worry-free when it comes to money are little kids because they don't know any better yet. Getting rid of your financial worries may not be easy, but what you can do is to have a good grasp of what your financial situation looks like. Once you've got a clearer picture, you can then set a proper plan and a budget in place. You'll feel a lot better when you've got a firm handle on your finances, and once you've crunched the numbers to put a proper financial plan in place – you can start working on improving your finances from there.

Not Having a Budget Is the Reason You're Still In Debt

The one thing we all have in common is that there *is* a reason behind why we have the debt that we do. Everyone has some experience with debt. Young, old, rich or poor, even if you've never experienced it firsthand for yourself, you're likely to know others who have been affected by it and seen what debt can do. The reason you never seem to make a dent in your debt is that you're *not* in control of your finances.

The problem is we love to spend *more* than we think about saving for the future. This dreaded mentality of *Keeping Up With the Joneses* is among the crucial reasons why so many find themselves in more debt than they should. If you keep going down the same road and spending money that you don't have, you'll soon be following in their footsteps and digging yourself a deeper 'debt hole' than you'd like. A lot of people struggle with the idea of making a budget because they're not willing to make sacrifices for the long-term. Making sacrifices is never something we would choose willingly if we could help it. Depriving ourselves of the joy that purchasing that cup of coffee each morning on the way to work brings, or the thrill of eating out several nights a week, can make the prospect of sacrifice a concept you're not willing to entertain.

Getting out of debt must become your priority right now if you hope to achieve financial freedom *before* you hit your retirement years. The longer you keep putting that off, the more debt you're going to accumulate. There will never be a 'good' time to start tackling your debt; the best time to do it is *now*. It's not going to be easy to make the necessary sacrifices, but it certainly will be worth it when you see your debt start to diminish.

When Should I Start Making a Budget?

The best time to start making a budget is *now*. That's right, not tomorrow, not next week, next month, or far in the future when you start earning more money. It's right now. There is no perfect time to begin this process. Instead of giving yourself excuses not to do this, *find the time* to sit down and assess your current financial state. This is often the most unpleasant portion of the process. Taking stock of your finances is frightening for some. It is not the salary that's the problem; it's your spending habits. When you consistently spend more than you make, you will continue to remain in debt and incur even more debt. Without a proper budget, curbing your spending habits will always be a constant struggle.

A budget encompasses everything from how much you're making per paycheck, how much you've accumulated in savings to date, and perhaps the most cringe-worthy one of all is how much debt you need to pay off. It may make you wince, but this step of the process is necessary because when you've got an accurate picture, you've got a better idea of what needs to change. Having this clarity of mind serves to bring you one step closer to your target of financial independence. If you happen to be in the middle of the month when you're reading this, that's okay. Start setting yourself up for next month, and in the meantime, try to limit your spending and cut back on your expenses as much as possible.

Deciding on a Budgeting System That Works for You

The method you choose is going to be based on how you get paid. Don't worry about trying to figure out your expenses just yet. The point of this step is to become familiar with the two methods of budgeting:

- **The Zero-Based Budget -** This is for those who get paid each month consistently with the exact same amount in every paycheck. This system is going to help you budget every single dollar of your income *before* the month even begins. This way, all of your income is accounted for and has a specific place to go from the moment it enters your bank account. At the end of this budget, you should have $0 left from your paycheck as every cent should have been directed to a specific task.

- **The Irregular Income Budget -** Now, if your paycheck tends to vary, then this second budget approach is your best bet. This one lists all your expenses for the month based on priority. Basic needs like housing, food, and transportation are going to be at the top of your priority list. As you make your money throughout the month, you will spend that money based on your highest priority items and trickling all the way down to the lowest priority (entertainment, eating out, leisure). Since you're not sure how much money you'll be making exactly per month, you want to use your average take-home pay over the last few months as a starting point.

Setting Your Budgeting Goals

You'll need to figure out what's important to you to set your goals. Your goals are the reason *why* you wanted to start budgeting in the first place. Setting a goal will help you determine where and how you should be spending your money. If you're trying to pay off debt, then you'll need to have a little bit of money left over to go towards paying off those extra debt payments to reach this goal sooner. If you're trying to save for something specific or invest for retirement, then you'll need to have some money left over in your budget to direct towards *those* particular things.

Another reason why goals are important is their ability to solidify the idea of a reward or a happy outcome tied to the end of your budget. If you need to start telling your money where to go, then you need to figure out how much you have to work with. Take the time to list every source of income you expect to have each month. You may be eager to get started and try to save as much money as possible right away, but that's not the best way to go about it. Once you've completed the first step, you then need to set realistic savings goals based on your *current* situation. If you try to do too much too soon, you'll eventually burn out or not be able to keep up with your targets, and this only leads to feeling discouraged and possibly even giving up along the way.

Set realistic goals based on how much you can save at this point once your bills and debts for the month are paid off. Ideally, it's advisable to save about 20% of your paycheck as a starting point but adjust this number if it's something you're unable to cope with just yet. As your finances change, you can adjust your goals. The most important thing is that you're able to save at least something and be able to survive *without* digging into what you've put aside. One of the most common mistakes made by the vast majority of people is paying all their debts for the month, spending on the things they need or want to buy, and then only attempting to save whatever's leftover. This is the wrong way to go about it because if you're going to build wealth, you need to *pay yourself first* before doing anything else.

Whenever you get a paycheck or a sum of money coming in, saving 15-20% of that should take precedence over everything else. Save first, and then distribute what's left accordingly for necessary bills, and only once these are paid do you spend any of whatever is left over. This will mean you have to live well below your means, but think of the bigger picture – the financial wealth and freedom you want to accumulate – as the motivator that keeps you going. Regardless of your circumstances, coming out of a financial rut and ditching the lifestyle of living paycheck to paycheck is a goal that you need to achieve. Think about what your resources are and work towards:

- Getting out of debt
- Establishing a substantial nest egg for emergencies
- Saving for a specific big-ticket purchase
- Planning for your future and retirement

You know you want to get out of debt and save more money for your goals, but you're at a loss as to *how* to do it. When you look at the amount of debt you have staring back at you, 5 or 6 figures in debt seems almost impossible to pay off with the salary that you're earning right now. It isn't easy, and it's going to take a lot of hard work and discipline to get it done, but most importantly, it can be done. Your savings goal could be anything from a *short-term* goal that lasts 1-3 years or a *long-term* savings goal that lasts more than four years. Goals are going to vary with each person.

Start with a goal of how much you want to begin setting aside monthly to build up your savings fund. When you outline your goals, be as definitive as possible to give you a properly-outlined target to work towards. A broad goal of "saving money" is not enough; you need to go into details. A more *specific* goal of "Save $10,000 by the end of this year" makes it a more tangible target to work towards. Gradually, you should aim to increase that goal over time. However, avoid being too ambitious. You want to keep your goals and target as realistic as possible to avoid giving up halfway, so keep in mind to pace yourself and make sure you're not stretched too thin. Keeping tabs on those financial goals that you *do* successfully accomplish is just as important. The motivation and the thrill that you get when looking back on your past accomplishments is an integral part of what drives you to keep going. The feeling of having paid off and canceled multiple credit cards or seeing your bank balance flourishing because of your efforts. These little victories are now going to replace the 'high' you used to get from your spending sprees; only it will feel even better because they bring you *closer* towards financial freedom.

Setting a Budget That You Can Stick to

The *time* that you invest in setting up your budget, in the beginning, is going to be well worth it when you see just how far your money can stretch when you want it to. It's going to be refreshing to not constantly feel like you need to scramble just to keep your head above water. If you're tired of feeling stressed about money, this is the only long-term fix. Think of each dollar that you earn as a soldier in your army, battling the forces that threaten to take you away from your goals and retirement plan. You're the general of your bank account, and it is now your job to give every single one of your soldiers a *job* to do. Your battle plan? *A budget.*

Getting started on a budget you can stick to, doesn't have to be complicated at all. Here's what you can do to simplify the process:

- **Step 1: Knowing Your Income -** This one is easy enough. Knowing how much you can save and spend each month requires knowing *how much* you're taking home at the end of the day after taxes, insurance, 401K contributions, and other stuff. Your budget needs to be based on your *net income*, not your salary.

- **Step 2: Figure Out Your Fixed Expenses -** Determine what your *fixed* expenses are every month. These are the numbers that don't fluctuate or experience any dramatic change throughout the year. These include rent payments, mortgage payments, car payments, insurance, and other loans you may have. This is also an excellent time to ensure that you're creating a safety net to help you pay for these expenses, just in case there was an emergency.

- **Step 3: Figure Out Your Variable Expenses -** The bills that *change* based on usage; your phone, utility, and grocery bills are examples of expenses that tend to fluctuate each month. Flexible expenses like restaurant meals and clothes should also be included in this category.

- **Step 4: Determine What Is Really Important -** Creating a successful budget means taking a good, hard look at what you believe to be truly necessary. As much as you would like to think you *"can't live"* without the latest phone or gadget, this expense should fall under the "I would like to have" category. These are not a priority. You need to rank your expenses in order of importance and cut out the stuff that you don't *need*.

- **Step 5 - Follow and Review Your Spending Monthly -** Give your wallet a fighting chance by keeping an eye on your budget. Ensure that you're spending within limits *throughout* the month. It's easy for small things to quickly add up if you don't account for them. Establish a system that works for you to keep track of your expenses. A pen and paper. A spreadsheet. Budgeting apps. What you choose to go with is up to you.

A budget is a process that is going to take time and effort, but if you put these steps into place, what you'll be getting in return is well worth it. Don't be afraid to talk about it with your family and seek their support. You're entirely reinventing your finances as you know it, and it's going to help you if your family understands and gets on board. Use family discussion time to try and work towards building a few common financial goals that everyone can pitch in on and work towards together. Having that familial support proves essential during the times that hit you hardest, which can be weathered by encouraging each other to keep going.

Chapter 3:
Wants or Needs

The difference between your needs and wants is one of the most important financial skills you could learn. A *need* is something you must have to survive, like food, water, shelter. A *want* is something that's nice to have, but truth be told, you could still live without. Like a new t-shirt, for example, when you own several good pairs already.

Establishing your needs and wants is going to set you on the right path and help you stick to your budget this time around. If you've tried to set budgets before, but they never seemed to work, perhaps the key underlying factor was not having established a clear distinction between needs and wants.

A Thorough Understanding of Needs and Wants

Needs vs wants is budgeting lesson 101. Imagine that you're going shopping and you have a list with you. You read through it: a new handbag, a new pair of headphones, present for a friend, sunglasses... oh, and a coffee and donut... because why not? *But* you know that you have to pay your rent and the car loan *and* buy groceries. Sigh. What could you possibly do now?

The question to ask is: *Do I really NEED all these things?* When you're looking at your budget, it's essential to identify your needs vs your wants. Making this distinction is crucial because it's going to help you determine your spending priorities, stop you from impulse-buying and overspending. This way of thinking encourages more thoughtful purchases and leads to, yes, you guessed it... *saving money.* There are some needs that everyone shares, like food and shelter, but there are also other needs that aren't as obvious, like the *need* to make decisions that are best for you.

Let's say, for example; you're currently enrolled in a study course that will help you get ahead in your career. You *need* a new laptop to complete the assignments and coursework in order to complete your degree. You've got a colleague who is enrolled on the same course and would *LOVE* to have a new laptop even though their old one is working just fine. Your colleague still *wants* a new laptop, but they will hold off on that purchase for a while and keep saving for it. Your *wants* are there to make your life more enjoyable and comfortable, but they're not necessary for your survival.

Set aside some time to think about the things you actually need in your life as you're listing the items that are going to go into your budget. Your needs should *always* be your first priority, and your *wants* should come second. No exceptions. You can continue to live without your wants and still find ways to be happy, but you wouldn't be able to survive or function as well as you could without your needs. Everyone has different needs and wants, so it's vital that you *do not compare* your budget to anyone else's. It's not going to be the same, and what works for them might not necessarily work for you. If you must, use budgeting templates as a guide, but your budget still needs to be personalized to cater to your current lifestyle – that's the only way it's going to work.

The Trouble With Separating Yourself From Your Wants

The problem is that we live in such a consumer-driven society these days that it can be challenging to tell a *need* from a *want*. If you're going to be starting on any kind of financial journey or debt-free journey, this is a critical topic that you need to tackle and explore further. There have been far too many times where you've found yourself at the store and thought *I really need a new pair of jeans* or *I really need those shoes, they look amazing!* Temptation can be so hard to resist, and it is a genuine struggle that plagues a lot of people. If it weren't a problem, we wouldn't be struggling to stick to a budget, would we? Or run out of money before the next paycheck is due.

There is a theory in psychology called *Maslow's Hierarchy of Needs; it* argues there are five stages of human needs, and that these are responsible for motivating our behavior. In 1943, Abraham Maslow proposed this theory after studying "exemplary people," as he called them. Maslow's hierarchy is one of the most legendary ideas in psychology that is still widely discussed today. Maslow wanted to discover what made life purposeful for people when he set out to create this pyramid. Maslow created the pyramid to depict the five stages of human needs and divided them into the following:

- **Stage 1 - Physiological Needs.** Maslow believed that we all begin with a set of utterly non-negotiable needs. This includes the need to breathe, eat, drink, and sleep. When we have those needs met, we feel rested, our bellies are full, we become motivated by the next stage.

- **Stage 2 - Safety.** These are the needs we seek to protect ourselves from bodily harm and provide a sense of safety and security. We work to earn money, build resources, and seek our shelter to protect ourselves from danger. Once we're satisfied and feel safe enough now that all our needs have been met, we think about the next motivating factor.

- **Stage 3 - Love and Belonging.** This focuses on the more spiritual needs we have. We want to be close to family and friends. We want to belong to a society.

- **Stage 4 - Esteem.** We desire the need to feel like we are somebody that matters. We want esteem and respect from our peers. If you have money, you might buy a fancy watch that draws the admiration of others. If you've got a brilliant mind, you seek to create a new invention that is going to change the lives of many. We go to school, college, take self-development courses because we are now motivated to perform.

- **Stage 5 - Self-Actualization.** Maslow also believed that we are all driven by a need for self-actualization. He described this stage as *"living according to one's full potential and becoming who we really are."* Only when we have our needs met in the first four stages, do we finally reach the fifth and final stage. At this stage, we can do whatever we want. We can relax, donate to charitable courses, enjoy life a little bit more. We're pretty happy by this stage since our first four needs have been met successfully.

Part of the reason why Maslow's description of the basic human needs has been so successfully persuasive lies in its ability to capture a profound structural truth about our human existence simply. This pyramid reminds us that we cannot live in one category alone and expect to be happy. That is to say; we cannot forgo one need *in favor* of another. You cannot focus only on your spiritual needs and live your best life while forgoing your physiological and material needs. There has to be a sense of balance and priorities to help you ascertain what you should be focused on, especially when so many elements are vying for your limited attention and resources. In order to be whole, to be complete, Maslow believed that both the material and spiritual needs must be attended to.

The above is something to think about when you're preparing your budget. Being too extreme in one category while completely neglecting the other is not balanced, and it is not going to be a sustainable approach long-term. For a budget to be part of your lifestyle without feeling like a burden, it needs to give you a sense of balance by fulfilling your most important needs first while still leaving some room to spare for other needs that fulfill you. It's okay to budget for your *wants* now and then, but you must be exercising responsibility for your other areas of spending.

Being Frugal Isn't That Bad

A budget teaches you how to stop feeling overwhelmed and guilty about how and where you're spending your money by taking the first step towards owning your finances. Living frugally is not as bad as it sounds once you get comfortable with the idea. The key is to establish a sense of purpose. Once you know *why* you need to do it, you'll be a lot more willing to see it through. Once you stop trying to fight against it, you'll see that it wasn't that bad after all. Being frugal teaches its followers to get the most out of their money by being thrifty. Using coupons at the supermarket, scouring the Internet (or catalogs) for the best sales and deals, so you can save more by spending less. Trying to find the cheapest possible option, so you have more money leftover to be directed toward your goals. It is incredible what taking control of your financial life can do for you.

Having a budget will help you put your spending into perspective. Being responsible and taking control of your spending brings you that extra step closer to financial freedom. Instead of continually struggling every month to stay on top of your bills and spending, you'll be taking back control by being mindful of where your money is going. To be accountable for your spending habits is a responsibility which will lead to making more informed choices concerning your spending. Take a look at where your money is going right now, and if those areas of spending are not in line with your new budget priorities, cut them out and redirect those funds towards your savings or to paying off debt. Increasing your savings and putting more money aside than you could before will leave you with enough to put some aside for a rainy day and pay off any debts you've got.

Budgeting begins with a change in your mindset. It's the way you think about your finances that will make the most significant difference at the end of the day. Change your mindset first and foremost about borrowing or owing money, whether this is to a financial institution or someone that you know. Sure, you'll hear people talk about how they bought a new car because they got a great deal on it, or because the monthly payments were so low and it was simply too good an opportunity to pass up. But...are they really being smart about it? Not exactly. What they are trying to do is stretch out their finances as much as they possibly can by trying to secure the lowest monthly payments. They do it because they believe that living beyond their means is going to make them happy, even though it's a lifestyle which, if they're honest, they can't afford. Temptation is clouding their judgement – they're not thinking about needs vs wants.

List of Common Expenses

Now that it's been established that some expenses are going to be more important than others, it's time to get a clearer picture of *what exactly* your expenses are every month. Budgeting begins by cutting out all unnecessary expenditure, but before you can do that, you need to know *what* your typical costs each month are:

- **Living Expenses -** Rent or mortgage, homeowner's insurance, tax, electricity, other bills

- **Debts (Other Than Mortgage) -** Loans, credits, interest payable, installment purchases, credit cards.

- **Investments and Savings -** Security fund, Payment for children's future education, setting some money aside for a holiday.

- **Food and Drinks -** Home grocery shopping, lunch allowances at school for children, eating out.

- **Medical Expenses -** Medications, medical visits, dental treatment, other treatment, medical tests

- **Transport -** Public transport tickets, petrol, car wash, parking fees, vehicle inspection, insurance, car repairs, taxi costs

- **Cable and Internet -** TV license, phone bill, spouse or partner's phone bill, kids' phone bills, Internet, channel subscriptions

- **Clothing** - clothes, spouse or partner's clothes, kids' clothes, dry cleaning, detergents

- **Health and Beauty -** Cosmetics and toiletries, hairdresser/barber visits, beautician appointments, gym memberships, vitamins and supplements, sports equipment

- **Kids Expenses -** Fees for school / kindergarten / nursery, additional activities, school supplies, school trips, pocket money, toys

- **Leisure and Entertainment -** Little treats like going out and meeting friends, cinema, theatre, concerts, books, music, movies, magazines, sweets, alcohol and cigarettes, games and lotteries, holidays and trips

- **Self-Development -** Courses, training, studies, books, ebooks, audiobooks.

- **Other Expenses -** Paid software and applications, insurance, bank charges, taxes

- **Pets -** food, medical, grooming, toys

- **Miscellaneous Expenses -** Gifts and presents for children, a partner, or family and friends, birthdays, holidays, Christmas

This is a rough guide, of course, since everyone's expenditure for the month is going to look different. But establishing your needs and wants is going to help you design a budget that is not only realistic but also prioritizes the *right expenses* first. Knowing what you want and need each month is going to help you problem-solve when you need to make tweaks and adjustments to your budget. A thorough analysis and reassessment of your needs and wants is a step that many people tend to overlook as they tend to jump right in and get started on dividing their income for their budget.

Remember, if you can live without it, then it can wait. Always focus on what you *must* spend each month first before you start focusing on any other category; that's the easiest way to get started.

Budgeting As a Couple and a Family

Romantic relationships are one of the easiest money traps to fall victim to if you're not careful about how you manage your finances. Poor decisions, conflicting priorities with your partner, and even poor communication are potential causes of financial disaster. You need to be as serious with your money as you are with your relationship, if not more so because your money is your only means of survival when you need it the most. Being secretive about your finances, letting your partner shoulder the financial responsibilities for you, not setting reasonable spending limits just to please your partner or spouse, and being overly generous because you want to impress your partner, are among the most common mistakes that get made when there's no budget in place.

Financial troubles are the reason that a lot of relationships and marriages break down, but it's a problem that doesn't get talked about enough. A couple must have a money dynamic or system that works for them. If you don't already have an effective one in place, it's high time you sit down with your spouse and talk about it. Financial troubles could lead to a lot of stress, debt, arguments, conflict, and eventually resentment when you begin to blame each other for the monetary mess that you're in. Setting a budget is always a smart thing to do, and when you're developing a budget, it's important that each person sets aside a little bit of money for their *personal* savings account. Joint accounts are great for shared expenses between the two of you and that sense of unity in a relationship and marriage. Still, you should always maintain a separate his and hers account respectively, even in marriage. Take these different accounts into consideration when you're mapping out your budget. Always save for a rainy day; you really do never know when you might need it.

Why the necessity to have a budget of your own that comes out of *your* paycheck? Because you need to kick the habit of depending on someone else for your finances. Stay in control, know exactly where your money is spent, regardless of whether you're in a relationship or marriage. This is one of the most basic principles of money management, but one that many couples still overlook, particularly women. Avoid making it a habit to become dependent on your spouse or your partner financially. You must be able to take charge and manage your financial situations on your by yourself because in the event your spouse or partner is no longer around, you'll find yourself in a very difficult position without an idea of how to handle your finances.

While being in love and having someone to share your life with is indeed a wonderful thing (and a need, as per Maslow's pyramid), love can also be an all-consuming emotion. It *is* easy to get so comfortable in the warm embrace of love that you lose sight of your independence. Though you're now co-existing with another person, never lose sight of the personal financial goals you set for yourself before you entered into that relationship or marriage. You are still your own person, and while you may be in a relationship, each person remains an individual. You have your own passions and interests, and even personal goals that might be vastly different from that of your partner or spouse.

If you're raising a family, then a budget becomes even more of a necessity. Raising kids on a fixed budget, which will still allow you to save some money for their future and your own, involves carefully planning a strategy to keep your finances healthy. As a parent, you need to be prepared, and plan for your financial future for the sake of your child – having funds you can fall back on without the help of your spouse is crucial. If you've got kids to think about, their needs must now be factored into your budget. Before you had them, your budget was centered around your expenses and your spending patterns. Now that you have kids, readjust your budget to include *their* needs and necessities. Re-evaluate which areas of your budget you can adjust, so you can divert and allocate resources to the needs of your child without compromising on your targeted savings percentage. It may require a lot of sacrifice on your part, but building a stable financial future for both you and your child is well worth it.

To be able to save money each month consistently, whether you're single, in a relationship, or raising a family, you *must learn* how to prioritize needs over wants. Spending way too much money on the things you can do without or aren't as important is going to be disastrous for your savings and put your financial future in jeopardy. You need to be able to make it through each month without dipping into your savings at all. Only when you have the wiggle room to spend on little luxuries for yourself and your family *without* impacting your finances, can you go ahead and indulge.

Chapter 4:
Calculate Income
and Expenses

Fall in love with the idea of knowing where your money goes. Understanding your monthly expenses is perhaps *the most* crucial reason why you're creating a budget. If you want to get out of debt and stay out, you need to know precisely what is going on with the money that you're bringing in each month. Everyone wants to save money. We've even been taught from a very young age by our parents just how important it is to save for a rainy day. The whole reason we work hard is to make as much money as possible, but bills and daily expenses can quickly rob us of our hard-earned salaries and leave us with barely anything at the end of the month if we're not careful about how we spend it.

The only way that you're going to achieve financial freedom and watch your savings account grow is to *spend less and save more.* Earn more so you can *save more, NOT spend more* (the mistake that a lot of people make). Minimizing and cutting down your expenses where you can, and minimizing unnecessary costs is the best way to increase your savings over time. But minimizing and cutting down on luxuries can be a sacrifice that is hard to swallow for many. Is there a way to save money without it damaging too much of your lifestyle? You don't need to be a financial expert or the most frugal person on the planet to be able to stick to a budget with success. What you need to be is *smart* – be meticulous with your record-keeping, disciplined in sticking to your budget. It's essential you rely on great strategies that have proven to be effective, and make the commitment to adhere to these because this is going to be a journey that you'll need to be in for the long haul.

Assessing Your Money Habits

When calculating your income and expenses, there's something else you need to assess too — your *current money habits.* Saving money, cutting back, and being disciplined about your budget doesn't have to be a process that brings you misery, and deprives you of all the little pleasures and enjoyment in life. The only way all the effort you put into planning and preparing for your budget is going to work is if you *change your current spending and saving habits.* More to the point, you need to change the current relationship that you have with money if this is going to work.

Sticking to a budget must begin with your *desire* to do so. If you don't want it bad enough, it isn't going to work. It's always going to feel like a burden if you don't start shifting the way that you think about this entire process. That's why you need that yearning and desire to take control of your finances. When the desire is strong enough, your willpower to stick to that commitment will follow suit.

Change your relationship with money and the way you think, handle, and manage your money. Getting started is always the most challenging part of the process. Still, once you get into the swing of things, it gets easier and easier to save more and spend less, while still being able to do little things to save money daily without affecting your lifestyle too much.

Why You Need *to Track Your Expenses*

Pause for a second and think about the answer to this question: *How much money did you spend last month?* You may remember the big-ticket items like the $300 birthday dinner you treated your best friend to or the $500 workout machine that you're probably not going to be using as much as you should. But what about the little expenses that you forgot about along the way? What about the $50 in total you spent on the coffee runs you made on the way to work? The $100 watch you purchased because your colleague had one, and it looked so cool you *had to have it*. If your expenses are something that you haven't paid attention to before this, it's time to start. If you don't track your expenses, you're never going to be financially aware. Period. How will you maximize your savings if you don't know exactly how much you're spending on unnecessary items you don't really need?

It's time to rid yourself of the *Keeping Up with the Joneses* mindset because this idiom is the very thing that's responsible for us spending our money unnecessarily and being unable to save as much as we would like. If you want to start saving money seriously, it's time for a little self-reflection. Do you have to have the latest item on-trend just because everyone else around you does? Do you find yourself spending more than you can afford only to maintain a certain image you have among your peers? Is your home overflowing with stuff, but your savings account bone dry most of the time? Do you own many items that you cannot afford on a credit card, which is adding to your debt? If you can relate to two or more of these, you're guilty of *Keeping Up with the Joneses,* and it's time to break out of the cycle if you want to start adopting more positive financial habits moving forward.

You could talk about budgeting and planning and being financially savvy for weeks or months. Still, at the end of the day, if you fail to track the ins and outs of your cash flow, you won't be able to fully appreciate the power that comes with taking control of your finances. Tracking your expense is going to:

- **Open Your Eyes -** All those little outgoings that you never paid attention to can add up to a surprisingly shocking amount, but you wouldn't know this unless you're actively keeping tabs on them. Once your eyes have been opened, it's going to make you more mindful about where you put your money, and you won't be so quick to whip out your cash or card the next time you make a trip to the store.

- **You Gain the Power of Priority -** Distinguishing between your wants and needs is going to become a lot easier once you start tracking all your expenses. You'll be able to look at your list and confidently say, *"I don't need this"* or *"I can live without this for now"* in favor of the expenses that matter.

- **It Makes You Prioritize Value -** If you're not getting value out of your money, it's not worth spending on that item. This is something that you'll begin to appreciate once you start actively tracking your expenses. Your closets overflowing with clothes that you never use anymore. The drawer full of gadgets that still work well enough that you don't need new ones. Entertainment subscriptions that you don't use as much because you don't have enough time. If what you're spending on is not bringing you value or worth your dollars, you're not spending wisely.

- **It Points Out Expenses That Don't Fit In With Your Values -** Now that you've set your financial goals, tracking your expenses is going to point out which of your spending habits is not aligned with your newfound goals. If they don't fit in with your goals, then the expenses probably need to be cut out.

Allocating Money

Before you begin creating your budget, you will need two pieces of information: *Your income and your expenses.* Income generally comes from two types of sources. The first is the income that you earn from your job or any kind of work that you do. The second type of income could be income that you derive from your savings and investments. Some people may have a third or fourth source of income. Essentially, the income you earn encompasses the following:

- Your wages and salary
- Any compensation or bonuses and commission received
- Your primary job
- Your spouse's job
- Freelance or part-time work
- Interests and dividends earned from savings and investments
- Stocks, bonds, mutual funds, and any other financial products
- Real estate income
- Social security
- Insurance settlement
- Alimony
- Child support
- Inheritance
- Trust funds
- Hobbies (if you're earning an income from them)

Just like your income, your expenses could fall into broad categories too. The fixed and consistent expenses are the costs you pay every month, quarter, or year. Variable expenses are slightly harder to define since a lot of these include things you need regularly. Sometimes, unexpected expenses could pop up that you didn't foresee. However, the variable expenses are the ones you have more control over compared to your fixed costs. The latter's amount is unlikely to change, whereas the variable expenses are the ones you could find ways to cut back on. For example, housing and food are both considered necessities, but what you pay for rent or mortgage payments are set, while your grocery bill is not a fixed amount every time.

Spending money is unavoidable because we still need the essentials for survival. Food, clothing, shelter, everyday household items and costs, we need those to survive each day. What we can do, however, is to start reflecting on the non-essential items that we end up spending money on and, at the end of the day, realize we didn't need all that much after all. That's why the first exercise involved distinguishing between your needs and your wants before anything else. Keeping all your receipts and bank statements will help you discover what your actual spending habits are. If your statements are all online, go and download them if necessary. It would be best if you had an accurate picture of exactly what you're spending on *before* you can begin creating an effective budgeting system that is going to work for you.

To make creating a budget more manageable, you need to start by gathering all your financial records. The three essential documents you are going to need are:

- Your payslips
- Your bank statements (including yours and your spouse's)

You'll need your bank statements so you can go over them line-by-line and see precisely what you're spending on and which patterns emerge. Next, you will need to assign your income to a category in your budget for the month ahead. Gather your payslips and bank statements according to:

- Bank account
- Spouse/partner's bank account
- Cash
- Spouse/partner's cash
- Commissions or benefits (if any)
- Extra income (if any)

When allocating your funds, the following categories need to be included in your budget:

- Savings and investments
- Fixed expenses
  - Rent
  - Mortgage
  - Insurance
  - Internet bill
  - Phone bill
  - Entertainment subscriptions (Netflix, Hulu, Amazon Prime, Apple TV, Disney+, etc.)
  - TV License

- Variable expenses
  - Food and drinks
  - Medical expenses and medications
  - Clothing
  - Home maintenance
  - Transport
  - Health and beauty
  - Kids expenses
  - Self-development
  - Debts (other than mortgage)
  - Leisure and entertainment (eating out, going to the movies)
  - Gifts
  - Other expenses

Here's an example of what your personal monthly budget for your income and expenses would look like:

Personal Monthly Budget			
	Projected monthly income	**Actual monthly income**	**Total balance**
Income	$4 800,00	$4 805,84	$5,84
Spouse/partner's income	$3 600,00	$3 612,11	$12,11
Bank account	$0,00	$0,00	$0,00
Spouse/partner's bank balance	$0,00	$0,00	$0,00
Cash	$20,00	$32,16	$12,16
Spouse/partner's cash	$35,00	$31,12	-$3,88
Commission or benefits	$0,00	$0,00	$0,00
Extra income	$0,00	$0,00	$0,00
Total monthly income	**$8 455,00**	**$8 481,23**	**$26,23**

Living Expenses	Projected Cost	Actual Cost	Difference
Rent or mortgage	$3 600,00	$3 588,67	$11,33
Homeowner's insurance	$0,00	$0,00	$0,00
Electricity Gas Water and sewage Waste removal	$140,00	$142,97	-$2,97
Maintenance or repairs	$0,00	$0,00	$0,00
Tax	$0,00	$0,00	$0,00
Other	$0,00	$0,00	$0,00
Total	**$3 740,00**	**$3 731,64**	**$8,36**

Debts (Other Than Mortgage)	Projected Cost	Actual Cost	Difference
Personal loans	$0,00	$0,00	$0,00
Student loans	$0,00	$0,00	$0,00
Other credit	$0,00	$0,00	$0,00
Credit card	$0,00	$0,00	$0,00
Interest payable	$0,00	$0,00	$0,00
Installment purchases	$0,00	$0,00	$0,00
Other	$0,00	$0,00	$0,00
Total	**$0,00**	**$0,00**	**$0,00**

Investments and Savings	Projected Cost	Actual Cost	Difference
Security fund	$200,00	$200,00	$0,00
Investment account	$0,00	$0,00	$0,00
Retirement account	$0,00	$0,00	$0,00
Children's future education	$150,00	$150,00	$0,00
Holiday savings	$100,00	$100,00	$0,00
Other	$0,00	$0,00	$0,00
Total	**$450,00**	**$450,00**	**$0,00**

Food and Drinks	Projected Cost	Actual Cost	Difference
Groceries	$500,00	$470,00	$30,00
Lunch at work	$200,00	$180,00	$20,00
Lunch at school	$0,00	$0,00	$0,00
Dining out	$300,00	$270,00	$30,00
Other	$0,00	$0,00	$0,00
Total	**$1 000,00**	**$920,00**	**$80,00**

Medical Expenses	Projected Cost	Actual Cost	Difference
Medications	$30,00	$26,00	$4,00
Medical visits	$0,00	$0,00	$0,00
Dental treatment	$0,00	$0,00	$0,00
Medical tests	$0,00	$0,00	$0,00
Other	$0,00	$0,00	$0,00
Total	**$30,00**	**$26,00**	**$4,00**

Transport	Projected Cost	Actual Cost	Difference
Vehicle payment	$0,00	$0,00	$0,00
Car insurance	$0,00	$0,00	$0,00
Licensing	$0,00	$0,00	$0,00
Fuel	$0,00	$0,00	$0,00
Parking fees	$0,00	$0,00	$0,00
Car wash	$0,00	$0,00	$0,00
Vehicle inspection	$0,00	$0,00	$0,00
Maintenance	$0,00	$0,00	$0,00
Car repairs	$0,00	$0,00	$0,00
Public transport tickets	$260,00	$254,00	$6,00
Taxi fares	$50,00	$48,00	$2,00
Other	$0,00	$0,00	$0,00
Total	**$310,00**	**$302,00**	**$8,00**

Cable and Internet	Projected Cost	Actual Cost	Difference
TV license	$30,00	$26,25	$3,75
Phone bill	$70,00	$61,00	$9,00
Spouse/partner's phone bill	$70,00	$64,00	$6,00
Kids' phone bills	$0,00	$0,00	$0,00
Internet	$65,00	$64,00	$1,00
Channel subscriptions	$9,00	$8,99	$0,01
Other	$0,00	$0,00	$0,00
Total	**$244,00**	**$224,24**	**$19,76**

Clothing	Projected Cost	Actual Cost	Difference
Clothes	$100,00	$98,00	$2,00
Spouse/partner's clothes	$100,00	$120,00	-$20,00
Kids' clothes	$0,00	$0,00	$0,00
Dry cleaning	$70,00	$72,00	-$2,00
Detergents	$40,00	$37,00	$3,00
Other	$0,00	$0,00	$0,00
Total	**$310,00**	**$327,00**	**-$17,00**

Health and Beauty	Projected Cost	Actual Cost	Difference
Cosmetics and toiletries	$50,00	$48,21	$1,79
Hairdresser/barber	$90,00	$98,00	-$8,00
Beautician	$0,00	$0,00	$0,00
Gym memberships	$210,00	$214,00	-$4,00
Vitamins and supplements	$0,00	$0,00	$0,00
Sports equipment	$0,00	$0,00	$0,00
Other	$0,00	$0,00	$0,00
Total	**$350,00**	**$360,21**	**-$10,21**

Kids' Expenses	Projected Cost	Actual Cost	Difference
Fees for school/ kindergarten/ nursery	$0,00	$0,00	$0,00
Extracurricular activities	$0,00	$0,00	$0,00
School supplies	$0,00	$0,00	$0,00
School trips	$0,00	$0,00	$0,00
Pocket money	$0,00	$0,00	$0,00
Toys	$0,00	$0,00	$0,00
Other	$0,00	$0,00	$0,00
Total	**$0,00**	**$0,00**	**$0,00**

Leisure and Entertainment	Projected Cost	Actual Cost	Difference
Going out with friends	$300,00	$261,12	$38,88
Cinema	$0,00	$0,00	$0,00
Theatre	$0,00	$0,00	$0,00
Concerts	$0,00	$0,00	$0,00
Sporting events	$0,00	$0,00	$0,00
Books	$0,00	$0,00	$0,00
Music	$0,00	$0,00	$0,00
Movies	$0,00	$0,00	$0,00
Magazines	$0,00	$0,00	$0,00
Sweets	$0,00	$0,00	$0,00
Alcohol and cigarettes	$40,00	$38,00	$2,00
Games and lottery tickets	$0,00	$0,00	$0,00
Holidays and trips	$0,00	$0,00	$0,00
Other	$0,00	$0,00	$0,00
Total	**$340,00**	**$299,12**	**$40,88**

Self-Development	Projected Cost	Actual Cost	Difference
Courses	$0,00	$0,00	$0,00
Training	$0,00	$0,00	$0,00
Studies	$0,00	$0,00	$0,00
Books	$0,00	$0,00	$0,00
Ebooks	$10,00	$9,99	$0,01
Audiobooks	$30,00	$29,90	$0,10
Other	$0,00	$0,00	$0,00
Total	**$40,00**	**$39,89**	**$0,11**

Other Expenses	Projected Cost	Actual Cost	Difference
Paid software and applications	$30,00	$27,00	$3,00
Insurance (home/ health/ life)	$0,00	$0,00	$0,00
Bank charges	$0,00	$0,00	$0,00
Taxes (federal/state/ local)	$0,00	$0,00	$0,00
Other	$0,00	$0,00	$0,00
Total	**$30,00**	**$27,00**	**$3,00**

Pets	Projected Cost	Actual Cost	Difference
Food	$0,00	$0,00	$0,00
Medical	$0,00	$0,00	$0,00
Grooming	$0,00	$0,00	$0,00
Toys	$0,00	$0,00	$0,00
Other	$0,00	$0,00	$0,00
Total	**$0,00**	**$0,00**	**$0,00**

Miscellaneous Expenses	Projected Cost	Actual Cost	Difference
Gifts for children	$0,00	$0,00	$0,00
Gifts for a partner	$30,00	$30,00	$0,00
Gifts for the family	$20,00	$20,00	$0,00
Gifts for friends	$10,00	$10,00	$0,00
Birthdays	$15,00	$15,00	$0,00
Holidays	$0,00	$0,00	$0,00
Christmas	$30,00	$30,00	$0,00
Other	$0,00	$0,00	$0,00
Total	**$210,00**	**$105,00**	**$0,00**

Summary of Personal Monthly Budget			
	Total income	Total expense	Total balance
Total projected (summary of all projected income, expense and balance)	$8 455,00	$7 054,00	$1 401,00
Total actual (summary of all actual income, expense and balance)	**$8 481,23**	**$6 812,10**	**$1 669,13**

Spreadsheets and templates like these can be created easily in Microsoft Word or Excel, depending on your preference. You can even create a customized spreadsheet of your own. This is merely a guide, showing you what should be included when mapping out your income and expenses for the month.

Please remember to download the free gift attached to this book with a Simple Budget spreadsheet.

Your categories should rank by order of *most* important, and trickle down to your *least* important categories. You'll get a much better overview of where you can afford to be cutting back and where you should be directing more of your funds. Creating your budget templates in Excel or Word makes it much easier for you to edit and adjust your different categories as you go along.

Keeping Your Records

Keeping track of your income and expenses is an absolute must, both for budgeting and for tax purposes when the need arises. Keeping track of every record in detail might sound like a tedious affair, but you'll be glad that you did it. Here are some tips to help you stay on top of your record-keeping all year long, so it doesn't feel like a massive, overwhelming task:

- **Have A Designated Storage Space for Your Receipts -** Have a specific drawer or folder just for your receipts. Knowing exactly where you put it and where to find it when you need it, makes it much easier when it comes time to record it.

- **Categorize Your Receipts -** Once you've found a designed spot in your home specifically to keep your receipts, make your job even easier by sorting these receipts into specific categories. Have one file folder for groceries, electric bills, water bills, pet supplies, household repairs, internet, phone, and the list goes on. Organize your receipts in the file folders according to date too, since organizing them in chronological order makes it easier for you to quickly refer to something specific when you need it.

- **Go Through Your Receipts and Expenses Once A Week -** Instead of leaving everything to the last minute, be sure to set some time aside where you can go through your receipts for the week. You could do this during the weekend, for example. Make records in your budget as you go along. This way, you have less to do at the end of the month and planning your budget for the next month becomes hassle-free.

Quick Tip: If you're constantly losing and misplacing your receipts even on quick trips to and from your home, a good idea is to carry a ziplock bag with you whenever you're out running errands, purchasing supplies, or doing any activity that requires spending money. As soon as you've collected your receipt, simply pop it into your ziplock bag – you'll know exactly where to find it. You can keep these ziplock bags in your purse, bag, car, or at the office, and that way you're sure not to lose them.

Quick Tip: If you're feeling stressed about the idea of tracking your expenses, start small by taking it one step at a time. Making spending changes can be a big deal, especially for those of you who have grown accustomed to spending without a second thought. Changing your spending habits does inadvertently involve changing the way you do things, and if you try to do too much too soon, you could end up stumbling and falling.

Chapter 5:
Create a Budget

Want to retire by the time you're 40? Planning to take that dream vacation you've been putting off for so long? You can do all of those things and more once you start disciplining yourself to stick to the budget you've created. Each time you feel yourself faltering in the process, reflect on your goals, and think about how good it's going to feel when you've reached them. Think about the effort you've put in so far and what a shame it would be to give up all that progress.

You've already done the hard part, which is *doing something about your finances.* You've finally realized that action needs to be taken, and you should feel *so proud!* The first step in fixing any kind of problem is to realize there is one, and you've *done that!* You just need to keep moving forward, slowly and steadily, one foot in front of the other. The next move to make is to sit down and put your budget together, once you have distinguished your needs and wants and gathered your bank statements. But first, let's go over your financial goals again, so these are crystal clear to you before you proceed.

Defining Your Goals With Clarity

Budgeting is not going to be much fun if you don't have an idea of *where* you want to go. It's going to be like driving in the dark. You're not going to be making much progress without a destination point in mind. Your budgeting destination points are your goals. How many times in the past have you thought to yourself; *I need a budget,* and started off enthusiastically only slip back into your old ways? That can happen when you don't have a definitive goal in mind.

As with anything in life, it is a lot easier to attain something when you have an end goal in mind. A purpose that you're working towards. Some examples of goals that would motivate you to stick to a budget include:

- Saving money to buy a house
- Putting money into your retirement account
- Paying off debt quickly so you can live debt-free

- Save for an emergency fund
- Save for your kids' college education

If you have a spouse, sit down with them and talk about your financial goals together. Work as a team because you're in this together, and you need to be on the same page. Talking money is not going to kill your relationship. The stress and anxiety that comes with dealing with debt will. If you're not talking about your income, bad spending habits, financial goals, and debt to pay with your significant other, you should be. Whether you're married or not, debt is going to put unnecessary pressure, especially in a marriage when a lack of financial security could well affect your spouse and the future of your kids. Disagreements can quickly lead to full-blown arguments, and eventually, the breakdown of the marriage if it goes on for too long. This can all be easily avoided if you take your finances seriously and start budgeting seriously. Your budget should be an accurate reflection of the goals you have for your finances, which is why you *need to know what those goals are* before you can even begin a budget.

When you are very clear about why you're doing something, it gives you focus and clarity. It makes you feel even more passionate about achieving it because you *want it badly enough*. When you set a goal, make a commitment to yourself that you are going to see it through to the end. Make it a promise to yourself. Think of each goal as a contract between you and your finances. Contracts are binding, and so should your commitment to your goal be. Every action that you take, even if it's a small one, should bring you one step closer to your goal. Every day brings you a little further, so never allow yourself to get discouraged by the setbacks you encounter. Challenges are a part of this process; there is no one out there who doesn't face a challenge or two when they are attempting to budget for the very first time. To make your goals even clearer, choose to write them down or organize them on a vision board, so you never lose sight of what you're trying to accomplish. Writing down your goals allows you to better assess and revise them as you take the necessary steps to make them a reality.

You'll be tracking your progress every step of the way, and at the end of each week, you can look back at the details and notes which you have written down to see what progress has been made thus far. Writing down your goals gives you a sense of direction, and it also helps you identify which areas you need to focus on or reassess. This makes it a much better tracking system than merely storing all the information in your head in hopes you won't forget it; there's too much going on.

Choosing a Budgeting Method

Some people might prefer to manually track their expenses in an Excel sheet since it's easier to make adjustments to it. Others might be more comfortable going with the pen and paper method and creating a fancy budget journal for themselves. Many people prefer the digital approach; we're constantly on our phones anyway, and there's an app for just about anything these days. There is no right or wrong here, choose the method which is the best *for you* when it comes to creating a budget.

If you do happen to prefer the digital approach, consider the following apps:

- **Mint -** This app has one of the most accessible user interfaces and makes the budgeting process very easy for those who are just starting out. You have the ability to set up categories with this one, so you can set a designated purpose for every dollar. The app allows you to link your bank and your credit card accounts, so they automatically import your transactions for easy budgeting. It pulls in all your recent transactions, so you don't have to enter those manually.

- **Digit -** A fully automated app that is great to help you with your savings. This hands-off approach is less stressful, and what is great is that it helps with building up your savings, quietly working in the background. You need to connect your bank account to the app, and Digit will analyze your spending patterns and locate smaller cash that can be saved. Ideal for people who have a problem managing to stash cash from their paycheck into a savings account. Every few days, the app automatically transfers cash into your Digit account, and when you do need the money, Digit transfers it back within one day.

- **Smart Budget -** This app is perfect for those with joint finances, and if you want to easily get a snapshot of your expenses and spending on a daily or weekly basis. However, the Smart Budget doesn't have features to set limits and doesn't feature budgets over multiple accounts.

- **You Need A Budget (YNAB) -** You'll get notified for all new transactions and when you have exceeded your budget in a category. The great thing about YNAB is the notification *will not go away* until you take care of the problem, which really encourages you to stay on point with your budget. It also makes the leftover amount for each budget category roll over into the next month by default, but this only works for positive amounts. This helps to promote savings and see where you're accumulating money for future purposes.

The 50/20/30 System for Beginners

If you're really struggling with getting started on creating a budget, don't worry, there is always a solution to work around it. If you need some guidance until you've found your footing and have a better idea of what your financial values and priorities are, you could begin your minimalist budget using the *50/20/30 System*. You're going to allocate 50% of your income towards meeting your monthly needs. A further 20% of your income is then going towards your savings and paying off your debt. The remaining 30% of your income is going to be allocated towards your wants. The latter is going to significantly decrease as you become more and more disciplined with your budgeting. This is a good guideline for beginners to start with.

The Recipe for
a Successful Budget

Once you're clear about how much money you're bringing in consistently each month (after tax), and you've gone over your bank statements for the last three months, made a record of every dollar you've spent, and segmented those into categories, this is what you need to do next:

- **Categorize -** Arrange all your expenses from most important to least important (this has been mentioned a few times in the previous chapters for a reason). Your expenses *need to be* in a hierarchy from the most important to the least important, so you *never miss another important payment moving forward.* This trains you to be disciplined to pay off your most important bills first, the ones you need to pay to sustain your lifestyle. Your rent or mortgage payments should be the number one priority on your budget list, followed by your savings and investments. It's equally important to pay yourself first *before* you start paying off your debt.

- **Decide On A Method -** Whether you choose to go with an App, do it old school using pen and paper, or go with an Excel spreadsheet, choose a budgeting method that is going to work best for you and *stick* *to it.* Avoid switching and changing your methods because this will only make the whole process messy and confusing in the long run.

- **Set Your Budgeting Boundaries -** Give every dollar a designated place to go from the beginning of the month. Set boundaries and limits when it comes to your expenses. Making a promise to yourself that you will not exceed the limits you have set. After taking a look at the last three months' worth of expenses, you should have some idea of how much you to allocate per category in your budget. The fixed costs are easy since the amount has already been decided for you, but for more variable expenses, set a realistic limit for yourself and commit yourself to not exceeding that limit.

Once you've completed the above steps, your budget's focus is now to tell your money *where to go.* This is much easier to do if you're on a fixed income, but even on a fluctuating income, these are the most important categories that your budget absolutely must address:

- **Saving for Retirement -** A true horror story would be running out of money before you die. This is a very depressing idea, and what's even worse is that it happens to so many people. Most of the time, it could have been easily avoided with better financial planning; although yes, it is impossible to predict what is going to happen in the future. Dave Ramsey, one of America's most trusted sources when it comes to all things financial, weighs in on this topic on his website, he points out that for a long time, there was a 'dream retirement financial number'. With $1 million in retirement, you could live out your retirement dreams and even leave an impressive legacy behind. That was back then. Today, even a million dollars may not be enough to lead that same lifestyle. Aim to save at least 5-15% of your income into a special retirement fund (this is something that should be accounted for in your budget).

- **Set Up An Emergency Fund -** This is going to be a separate account from your retirement fund. Things like clothes, a new phone, new shoes, can wait until you've paid yourself in your emergency fund first. If you don't have one, you need to set one up *right now*. Ideally, you'll want to have at least $1,000 in an emergency fund stashed away in an easy to access account. Start tucking away any spare cash you can find, and once you have accumulated at least $1,000, put it into a bank account – that's your emergency fund. Start putting funds aside little by little from your monthly budget until you have accumulated that amount. It's recommended that you keep these emergency funds in a separate account to all your other funds because you don't want to risk accidentally using it up and suddenly finding yourself with no money. This is why you should keep all your savings in a separate account, and do the same for your emergency fund. Top up that emergency fund each month and let the money accumulate until such a time when an actual emergency arises. You'll be so thankful that you have something to fall back on if and when you need it, so make that emergency fund column integral to your budget.

- **Set Up An Emergency Sinking Fund -** It's a good idea to include an emergency sinking fund into your budget allocations. A sinking fund is specifically for planned expenses that you *know* are coming up, like new tires of your car, for example. Creating a specific fund for those big-ticket items ensures that you don't have to dip into your savings or emergency fund to cover them.

- **Your Automated Savings -** Have a fixed amount in your budget specifically set up for automated savings and put it down as a recurring expense. Automating your finances saves you time, effort and takes away the stress of saving, as money simply gets taken out of your account as soon as your salary comes in. You don't even have to think about putting it aside – it's already been done for you!

- **Debt Payoff** - Once you've automated your savings, saved for retirement, saved to your emergency fund and paid all the essential expenses for the month like your rent, groceries, mortgage, and utility bills, it's time to direct some of your funds toward paying off your debt. One approach to paying off debt that has become popular in recent years is the *Debt Snowball Method*. Dave Ramsey, the advocate of this method, believes that it's one of the very best ways to get yourself out of debt quickly in the shortest amount of time possible. Just like the snowballs, you used to build as a child would gain traction as you rolled around your yard – what started as a tiny, compact snowball quickly grew into a giant boulder as it gained momentum and speed. This is how paying off your debts is going to work when you apply this approach – aptly named because it leads to gained momentum the longer you keep it going.

Upon examining your budget, you'll discover some pretty obvious places you could be cutting back your spending; purchasing that cup of coffee every morning on your way to work, for example. Homemade coffee tastes just as good *and* is a lot cheaper. Budgeting usually takes about three months of solid practice before you really start to get the hang of it. If your first month goes terribly and nothing goes according to plan, don't be too hard on yourself. That's okay, give yourself time to learn the ropes, and make adjustments to your lifestyle, take what you've learned and apply that to the next month.

Give yourself a grace period; you're learning how to budget for the first time after all. You don't have to do it perfectly right from the very first month; this is an entirely new process for you. Once you've made a monthly budget for yourself, you've got to stick to it. It all comes down to planning. Anyone can live on virtually any income if you know how to make every dollar count for something. It might even be fun to turn it into a challenging little game to see just how far you can make your dollars stretch every week. If you want to live well for less, it's an absolute must to have a budget. Having one and sticking to it is the winning combination. You may have previously associated the word 'budget' with restriction, but stick to one long enough, and you'll realize that a budget actually gives you *permission to spend*. Use your budget to accomplish your financial goals and enable you to enjoy life. A budget is your guide, and it allows you to live the life you want by holding you accountable. At the end of the day, a budget is a method that ensures you're paying all the necessary expenses first *before* moving to the unnecessary.

Bonus Tip:
Creating a Debt Snowball Method Spreadsheet

With each balance you successfully cross off your list of debts, your momentum increases. With the money that was previously allocated towards paying the smallest quantity of debt in full, is now out of the way, that money can be rolled over to the next debt that needs tackling. You can now make even larger payments in order to quickly demolish this debt too before moving onto the next, and so on. The method is simple enough to follow; it involves three major steps:

- **Step 1 -** In an Excel spreadsheet, you need to list down all the debts that you have, from the smallest amount to the largest (do this regardless of the interest rates involved).

- **Step 2 -** Target the smallest debt that you have first, and then aggressively work to pay that off while continuing to make the minimum payments on the rest of your debts. Any extra income that can be spared should be channeled towards paying off the smallest debt first until it's over and done with.

- **Step 3 -** Repeatedly work through this process, and you'll continue to smash through debts one at a time, till they're utterly decimated.

With the debt snowball method, you want to attack the debt with the lowest balance *first*, and only then tackle the debt with the second-lowest balance. You can then progress to the next and work your way up from there.

Chapter 6:
And Action!

If you don't learn how to make your money work for you, you're always going to be a slave to it. A budget is a plan, and with a plan, you can accomplish anything. It's only a matter of time before you reach any financial goal you've set yourself once you have the discipline and commitment to stick to it. Now that you've established the budget system that you would like to follow, the next step is to follow up on the process with regular reviews.

Why Review Regularly?

Planning your finances can be an intimidating process, and reviewing them to see how well you've done can be just as stressful. We don't want to see the mistakes we may have made. We don't want to kick ourselves in the butt, thinking we could have done better when we see where we went wrong. People, in general, do not like to confront mistakes because mistakes are seen as a weakness. The first few months of your budget can be challenging, but keep trying to get everything in line until you're able to follow it perfectly. Perhaps it's even a little intimidating to make all these significant changes to your spending habits. You want to do the right thing by saving, planning for the future, and getting out of debt. Yet, at the same time, you want to have some fun and make sure you're enjoying yourself a little after working so hard to support yourself throughout the month. How do you do all the things that you desperately want to do *and* still keep your spending plan on track?

You do so with *regular budget reviews*. How often should you be conducting these reviews? A major review can be undertaken once every six months, but at the end of the month, a quick review is still in order, so you can check if any category needs to be adjusted. A monthly review is helpful to see if you're on track and course-correct as you go along, so you don't veer too far off from your goals. Think of your budget review like your employee performance review at work. The reason your boss conducts those regularly with you at work is to track your performance and help you to boost it. It's the same thing with budget reviews. You want to conduct these reviews regularly to track how well you're doing and strengthen your financial performance.

The Best Way to Conduct Your Budget Reviews

The most effective kind of review is one that is done regularly and consistently. It allows you to figure out *what you need to do* to be better. With a budget review, you get instant access to how well you're performing. You don't have to *guess* or *think* that you're doing well. A review lets you know exactly where you stand.

The best way to conduct a review is to:

- **Schedule It -** Treat every review session seriously and make an appointment with yourself to analyze your budget. Schedule your review sessions the way employers schedule performance reviews: choose a specific date and time. Note it down on your calendar, so you don't forget it, and doing so cements the idea in your mind, and reinforces the importance of taking your budgeting seriously.

- **Relax -** Looking at your finances can be stressful, so do what you can to calm yourself down before you sit and begin going over your budget. Put your mind at ease by reflecting on your goals and reminding yourself there is a *good* reason why you have to do this. Go for a walk to clear your head beforehand, make yourself a nice cup of coffee, meditate, do anything that makes you feel relaxed and comfortable, so you're not in a stressed-out state of mind when looking at your numbers.

- **Think Of This Review As A Positive Thing -** The way you choose to perceive things is going to make a big difference in the way you approach anything in life. Any challenge can seem monumental and impossible if that is the mindset that you choose to have. You've been resistant to the idea of budgeting all this time, probably because you've had a negative perception associated with it. But once you change that mindset and see it through a positive lens, focusing on the benefits it brings rather than how much you're having to cut-back and sacrifice; suddenly budgeting doesn't seem so bad after all. Reviewing your budget works along those same lines.

- **Evaluate Each Category -** Evaluate each category and review how well you did at sticking to the budget that you set. Compare that to the goals that you set when you first implemented the budget. If you identified any gaps in your spending, this allows you to figure out not only why, but what can be done to get you back on track before you slide further. Evaluating each category is an opportunity to see your triumphs too, and seeing the progress you made encourages you to keep going - you have clear visual proof in front of you that you are more than capable of handling it.

- **Summarize Your Commitments -** After reviewing your budget, summarize the commitments you want to make for next month's budget. That way, each month, your budget gets progressively improved upon compared to the last. Finally, don't forget to calendar in the next review session, so you ensure you're treating these reviews as a serious commitment.

Budgeting Mistakes and What You Should Be Doing Instead

Budgeting is the single greatest tool you could have to reach your goals and stay in control of your finances at last. As in any journey, there are few bumps and hiccups along the way that a new budgeter like yourself might encounter. A budget stops you from 'upgrading' your lifestyle with each pay rise you get. Bonuses, tax refunds, extra income is all money that should technically be put aside towards your savings fund, yet most people's thoughts jump straight onto what they should treat themselves to. *That* ends up being how the dangerous cycle of living paycheck to paycheck is born. Even if you already know the importance of having a budget, or you've had one for a while, and you're loving what it is doing for your finances, you could *still* be making critical mistakes that are throwing off your entire spending plan. So, we need to take the time to look at some common budgeting mistakes and how they can be avoided or fixed.

One crucial mistake that gets made when budgeting is not reviewing that budget regularly. Your budget is not something that you can set and forget. Over time, your income and expenses are going to change. There's going to be an increase or a decrease; when this happens, you will have to make adjustments to your budget. This is particularly important if your income drops because if you are bringing less money in, but not making any adjustments to your spending, you are on your way to digging a deep hole for yourself: you may not have enough money for your needs. At this point, you might feel like you have to take savings out of the equation altogether, and depending on how deep into the hole you are, you might even feel like you have to use a credit card to keep your head above water. You *need* to review your budget from time to time. If your expenses go up in one category, you may need to reduce how much you are spending in another to keep everything in balance.

- **Using Your Gross Income -** One mistake that you want to avoid when you're reviewing your budget is to make sure that you're not using your gross income. For any budget to work, your starting point needs to be your *after-tax income.* It's just not going to work if you take your annual salary, divide that by 12 and use this figure as a starting point. Doing this means you're *overstating* your income, and on paper, it will trick you into thinking you have more money than you actually do. When you think you have more money than you do, there's a very good chance that you're going to overspend every month. So remember when you're reviewing your budget, it's not the *gross salary* that you're looking for, but the figure that you're bringing home *after taxes* and *after payroll deductions.* That's the figure that you want to be working with.

- **Guessing our Monthly Expenses -** Figuring out your actual income is one part of creating a budget that works. The second part is having an *accurate* portrayal of your expenses... this is where a lot of people tend to go wrong because instead, they *guess* their monthly expenses. You want your budget to be as accurate as possible, and if you're guessing, that's already far from accurate. Guessing can lead to overstating or understating your expenses, and if you don't have a clear picture of how much money is leaving your account each month, your budget is going to start off on the wrong foot. This is why you need to take a good look at your expenses over a period of 3 to 6 months, to know precisely how much money is leaving your account and where that money is going. When reviewing your budget, it's your bank statements, credit card statements, bills, and receipts that are going to be your best friends - with these you have proof of exactly how much you're spending. Of course, you need an accurate figure for how much you're spending on your fixed expenses, but you need to account for your variable expenses too.

- **Spending Too Much In One Category -** Another reason why it's essential to review your budget regularly is to observe if you're spending far too much in one particular category. The 50/20/30 method is ideal for a first-time budgeter because it stops you from overlooking or forgetting to budget for savings. The 50/20/30 method works because it gives you a specific breakdown of how your income should be divided. If you keep your needs, wants, and spending within these percentages, you're almost always guaranteed to have money left over that you could then put into your savings account or towards your debt repayment.

- **Forgetting About the Irregular Expenses -** Reviewing your budget is necessary to avoid the mistake of overlooking your irregular expenses. For the expenses that might come up only quarterly or annually, instead of reaching for your emergency fund, it's best to gradually save for these expenses throughout the year and put this money in a *separate* savings account. That way, when the time comes to pay it, you're not caught off-guard. To include irregular expenses into your budget, gather information about the expenses you've paid in the past, get a number, divide it by 12, and then set aside that much every month, so you're prepared. When it's time to pay these expenses, you'll have the money on hand with no need to dip into your emergency fund to do it!

- **Not Budgeting On Paper** - Tracking your budget in your head might be a workable solution for some, but it's always better to get it down on paper. When you don't have a visual, it becomes all too easy to lose track of your spending at some point during the month. If you lose track of your spending, there's an even greater likelihood of overspending, and once the overspending starts, your whole budget gets thrown off track. By the end of the month, you could come up short, maybe dip into your savings to pay a bill, pay a bill late, or worse, feel like your only option is to pay your bill with a credit card, which is never a good idea. It doesn't matter if you choose to use a spreadsheet or a budgeting app, just so long as you have a visual of where your money is going, that's all that you need at the end of the day.

- **Thinking You No Longer Need A Budget After A While -** Once you've got your debt in order and you're back on track with your finances, it's easy to believe that you don't need a budget anymore. You've done it, you've got your finances in check, and you're confident that you can keep it up moving forward. Unfortunately, that is not always the case. Regardless of your income level, let's say even if you're a millionaire or billionaire, *there is always a risk of overspending.* We've all heard one too many horror stories about millionaires and rich people who had it all and then lost it all, and we wonder how it went so horribly wrong for *them.* In all likelihood, it's because they didn't have a budget that they were sticking to. Not having a budget is the crucial reason why people could be making good money every month, yet still find themselves living paycheck to paycheck. Giving up your budget after you've grown to feel more secure is going to be one of the biggest mistakes you could possibly make. Your budget is the game plan for your money and a way to ensure that you always have enough for the things that you need. You should *always* have a budget with you even when you're well into your retirement years. Without a budget, you're always at risk of overspending, and when you overspend, you're going to end up back where you started: in debt and living paycheck to paycheck.

Strategic Budgeting for Retirement

If you can implement a budget and commit to sticking to it before you retire, you will have a lot less to worry about when the time comes as opposed to someone who has been operating without a budget for years. Retirement may seem like a distant thing at the moment, but you never know when things could change or when you could be forced into early retirement. It's never a good idea to wait until the last minute before taking action, and a regular review of your budget is essential to ensure you're well on track toward preparing for your golden years *before* they happen. Given your age, family history, and current health and medical status right now, work out a plan of how much you are going to need to live comfortably each year. Since there's no way of finding out just how long you will live, it's best to plan for as far ahead as possible, maybe even well into your 90s.

The budget plan for your retirement should be focused on the kind of retirement lifestyle you intend to lead. This would depend on where you plan to live and how your plan to live once you retire. For example, if you were planning to retire in a nursing home, eventually, you would need to prepare enough financial resources to cover those expenses. If you've already had certain activities in mind which you want to get involved in upon retirement, you would need to plan for those accordingly. All this planning must be done when you're still in the working stage of life, and every budget review should ideally take this into consideration. Budget reviews help you ascertain whether you're still progressing in the right direction towards your goal, and in case you're wondering, *it's never too early* to start budgeting for retirement. In fact, the sooner you do it, the better prepared you will be since it gives you enough time to save up for it *without* needing to dip into your other savings accounts.

When preparing your regular monthly budgets for the present, prepare for the future too, by looking into the retirement plan options which you are eligible for and can start investing in as soon as you can. If you're working for an employer, have a chat with your manager to see if you're eligible for the company's retirement plan. The sooner you start, the more you will be able to save. Budget for those savings and work them into your *current* spending patterns.

Once you've got your finances under control, having budgeted consistently for a couple of months, it's time to think about opening another savings account specifically for retirement healthcare. It seems by this point that a lot of your salary is being directed towards savings, but you'll be glad of it in future. Fulfilling your current wants won't seem as important when you're strapped for cash during retirement with no way to pay for your healthcare. Healthcare can be a massive drain on your finances, especially since you're going to be needing a lot more of it as you get older. You've got your long-term health insurance to help you out in that department, but you also need to take control of the situation by creating a separate savings account for yourself for should there come a time when you need it.

Financial independence will give you freedom and guarantees that you will not have to depend on your family members, children, spouse, or partner to care for you in your old age. Think about how good it's going to feel when you: no longer have to rely on banks, loans, and buying things on credit anymore, are able to go on vacation without having to rely on your credit card to do it, can survive the month comfortably instead of counting the days to your next paycheck. Money and control over your finances is the key to a free life, but only if you're using it right. To evolve from a spender into a saver, you need to learn how to feel just as good about saving money as you do about spending it. The way to start nurturing this good feeling is to remember all the reasons *why*. No more purchasing first and then struggling to pay those monthly installments with high-interest rates. Just pick, pay, and you're done. That's what savings can do for you. Preparing financially for the future is one of the smartest financial decisions you will ever make, and the preparation begins right now.

Chapter 7:
How Should I Manage
Seasonal Expenses?

Those dreaded irregular expenses can be a *huge* budget-breaker if you don't plan for them well in advance. Some examples of these irregularities include housing repairs, pet bills, property taxes, holidays, auto maintenance, and a whole lot more depending on the kind of lifestyle that you lead. These expenses may only happen once in a while, but you still need to account for them when you're sorting out your budget.

Unfortunately, you don't have the luxury of forgetting about them when you're planning your monthly budget. Saving for these seasonal expenses consistently is the best way to ensure you're as well-prepared as you can be when the times comes.

The Problem With Seasonal Expenses and Keeping a Budget

Once you start keeping a budget for a few months, you'll begin to notice the problem with seasonal expenses when you're trying to juggle a limited budget. Sure, they happen only once or a few times a year, but they're still budget-busters as they can quickly throw an otherwise well-conceived budget into chaos without a proper strategy. The most problematic ones are the ones that incur the largest sums, of course. One proactive system to tackle the problem of seasonal expenses is to create a 'sinking funds' account.

What Is A 'Sinking Funds' Account

You could call it a reserve fund, holiday fund, whatever you'd like based on your preference. So what is a sinking fund exactly? Well, it's essentially money that you're going to be setting aside for either a planned or unplanned event. Unlike the rest of the money you're setting aside for savings, sinking fund money is going to be set aside *specifically for spending.* This is different from the emergency fund that you're setting up too; since an emergency may or may not happen. With a sinking fund, you *know* one or more of your seasonal expenses are coming, and these are the funds set in place to cover those costs. Like Christmas time, for example. We all know that Christmas comes once a year, and we know when it is going to happen, so what you can do is have a plan set aside to save money and have some funds available to you during that month.

Let's go with a basic example and say that you want to have $1000 set aside by the time Christmas comes. You should start figuring out as early as possible how much you should be saving each month so you can achieve that $1,000 target by December. If you plan to save little by little each month and budget for this with every paycheck you get, you're not going to be scrambling when the time comes to try and organize the funds for your Christmas expenses.

Now, expenses coming up once a year may not seem like a big deal, but when you have to dip into all that money you worked hard to save, it can do more than just put a dent in your savings account. It's going to hurt your motivation too. You're going to feel frustrated seeing the money you worked so hard to save run out in a matter of minutes. That sense of frustration and demoralization can lead you to feel as though it's pointless putting in the effort to save if it's just going to go to waste like that anyway. Irregular and seasonal expenses steal both your savings and your motivation.

Once you start losing that motivation, you begin to lose momentum too. You start to question why you've been working so hard only to end up in this horrible situation. You feel completely dejected, and you're wondering what you can do to keep this from happening again.

A Plan for All Seasons

Regular expenses are so much easier to budget for since they happen every month. It's the irregular ones that often get overlooked or forgotten. Without proper planning, it's easy for these seasonal expenses to put a big dent in your savings and budget. If you happen to charge one of your irregular expenses to your credit card with no immediate plan to pay it back, remember the interest is going to accumulate with each month that it is carried forward.

The first and easiest solution to handle your seasonal expenses is simply to plan ahead. Chances are, you already have some idea of what your seasonal expenses are. Luckily, this seemingly big problem has a simple solution:

- **List Your Irregular Expenses for The Year -** Make a comprehensive list of your irregular expenses and find out exactly how much you're spending per expense. You'll have to pull out your bank statements and receipts from the past year for an accurate estimate (remember not to guess the amount, or you could be at risk of over budgeting or underbudgeting). Once you have your list, add the total of each individual item to get a lump sum figure of what you should be saving for. Anything that you anticipate for the coming year put down on paper (or on your Excel sheet).

- **Open A New Bank Account -** This bank account should specifically be for your irregular expenses *only*. This is not your emergency fund, your holiday fund, your savings, or anything else. It is an account that should be dedicated to nothing except your seasonal expenses.

- **Dividing Your Lump Sum According to Pay Days -** Once you've got your lump sum figure and your bank account ready to deposit these funds, it's time to divide the final figure that you need based on the number of paydays that you have. If you get paid monthly, you would divide that lump sum figure by 12 to get the amount you should be setting aside each month. If you get paid bi-weekly, you would divide that lump sum figure by 26. One option you could go with is to open a short-term 'sinking funds' savings account, which is an account that you add to periodically.

- **Make Immediate Deposits -** As soon as you get your salary, the designated amount should be deposited into your new bank account without hesitation. *Never skip a payment either,* no matter how much you may be tempted because that seasonal expense still feels like it is so far away. Oh no, you need to start putting money aside *now* and let it accumulate in time for when the expense occurs.

- **Track the Ins and Outs -** Track the transactions that take place in your new bank account. This helps you stay on top of your spending in case you overestimated or underestimated a certain category.

- **Take Advantage of Seasonal Incomes -** Take advantage of any extra cash, commission, or bonuses that come in and use that as an opportunity to add to your funds. Maybe you got an extra-large tax refund or an unexpected bonus from work. Since this income was unexpected and probably not already included in your budget, you can take that money and set it aside for your irregular expenses.

- **Have A Strategy -** Once you have a strategy in place, like a monthly budget, for example, you can safeguard the rest of your savings that you worked so hard to set aside. Keep the emergency fund *only* for emergencies, and your savings only for a rainy day. If you know at some point that you're going to have to handle a seasonal expense, then the smart thing to do is to have a strategy in place to prepare for it. That strategy could be something as simple as being disciplined enough to stick to a budget, or having a few tricks up your sleeve to see which areas of your life you can afford to cut back on to save some money.

- **Don't Feel Bad About Using Your Funds -** If you have to use your funds from this seasonal bank account, don't feel bad about it. That is what those funds are there for. You don't need to feel bad about reaching into that sinking fund because that's *the whole reason* you set it up. They can always be replenished in preparation for the next time they come up.

How to Budget for Several Things on a Limited Income

By this point, it feels like you've got a lot on your plate that you need to juggle with (perhaps) a limited income. You've got to save for a rainy day, an emergency, your sinking fund, save for retirement, pay for your rent or mortgage, pay off your debt, and deal with a whole host of other monthly expenses. How do you do it all if your income is only so much? You're not running on unlimited funds, and even with a budget, it can feel like you're stretching yourself thin, so the solution, in that case, would be to see where you can afford to scale back a bit in certain areas of your life.

How do you save money as a renter? How do you scale back on your grocery, food, and clothing bill? After you've been working with a budget for a while, you'll begin to notice certain areas where you're spending when you could be saving. Let's look at some of these areas now and see how you can save yourself some money that could be channeled elsewhere for a greater good.

Saving Money When You're Renting

Saving money as a renter can seem like an impossible task, but it is surprisingly more doable than you think. Did you know that you could potentially be saving *more money* as a renter than a homeowner? Let's investigate that for a minute. Buying a home doesn't come cheap. Once you've bought your home, other expenses are going to crop up. You've got your recurring expenses, which would be your mortgage payments, condo or community living fees if you purchase a condo, maintenance, homeowners insurance, and property tax.

You need to look beyond the initial cost, which is the down payment that you're going to put down for your home and look at the other costs involved in purchasing a home.

As a homeowner, you'll need to factor in renovation costs which are coming out of your own pocket, the cost to furnish your home, and the cost of the ongoing maintenance that your home will require as the years go by, all of which you will have to bear because you are the owner of the home. Now, if you were to compare that to being a renter, the initial costs that are going to come out of your pocket when you opt to rent a place to live in simply include the rent security deposit, which, let's face it, is a lot cheaper than the cost of paying a down payment. Your recurring expenses here include your monthly rental, which includes heat, cable, water depending on where you rent or live, and your renter's insurance. If you're on a mission to save and bulk up your bank account, the choice is clear. Renting saves you a lot more money, especially for those who are lucky enough to score low rent places or rent-controlled buildings. Minimizing your monthly spending is how your bank account grows each month until you have reached a point where you're able to comfortably afford your own home while still having a substantial balance in your bank account.

As a renter, some quick tips on saving money to boost your savings are:

- To aim for a place that has the utilities and amenities built into the monthly rental payment, not as a separate expenditure. Combining both payments into one can save you quite a bit of money each month.

- Aim to rent a place that *you can afford realistically.* It can be tempting, especially when you're young, to live the kind of life we see on television. Don't fall for depictions on TV of those who can afford seemingly afford really pretty and fancy places to live, even on a tiny budget. As much as we would like that to be the case, the reality just isn't quite as pretty. Living in a smaller place that is just enough for your needs will go a long way in helping you save money.

- If you're one of those people that enjoys a good fixer-upper project, you can paint and handle repair works around a home without resorting to calling a handyman. You could use this useful skill to try and negotiate cheaper rent with the landlord in exchange for fixing things around their units.

- Rent as close to work as you possibly can because it saves you money if you can easily walk to work rather than having to spend money on transportation costs!

Saving Money on Food, Clothing, and Shopping

This is where the battle between our needs and our wants is at its strongest. How do we resist the urge to buy the things we're so tempted to buy and stay responsible? Everyone knows that if you want to save money on food, you need to forgo the luxury of eating out all the time. Preparing your own meals at home has been proven to be significantly cheaper, and if you're planning to get serious about saving money, this is the way to do it. As for shopping, well, shopping is the mother of all temptations. Too often, many of us have been guilty of spending more than we should on shopping trips because temptations and bargains are so hard to resist. We have all experienced (more than once) how a purchase seemed like such a marvelous idea at that time, but upon getting home, those feelings of regret and guilt started to creep in, and we kick ourselves for spending money unnecessarily.

So, how do you scale back in these areas without feeling the pinch too much, still leaving room in your budget for the more important things?

- Skip the frozen and pre-packaged foods. Yes, they seem cheap, and they're incredibly convenient, but if you take a good, hard, look at the ingredient list, and what you're actually getting for the price that you pay, it turns out it's not a very good deal at all. If you bought the ingredients yourself, you could get more value for money, plus it's much better for your health overall.

- Generic brands are great alternatives, and they come for a fraction of the cost. Generic brands are very often given a miss or overlooked by consumers because many believe that they are not 'as good' as the brand name products. When was the last time you remember seeing an advert for a generic or in-house store brand product? Probably never. This manner of thinking is nothing more than a marketing gimmick. Generic brands are just as good as their big-name competitors. They're much cheaper and better for your wallet, and if you find that you don't like the taste of a generic brand product, you can always switch back to the big-name brands you're accustomed to buying.

- If you live in a community that holds weekly farmers' market sessions, it's time to start frequenting them for more value for money. At farmers' markets, you'll find that the prices of produce such as fruits and vegetables are reasonable, and the products you get are much fresher than what you would find in a grocery store.

- Coffeeshops. As delicious and tempting as the coffee options are, they aren't good for any money-saving goal you have set for yourself. Calculate how much you spend on average in a Starbucks outlet, multiply that by a period of one year, looking at the numbers would probably leave you in a state of shock. It's much cheaper to brew your own coffee at home before you leave for work. If you spend on average $1-2 dollars brewing your own coffee at home, think about how much money you're saving just by doing that compared to what you would spend in a year at coffee outlets.

- Never shop during an emotional rush, whether you're happy or sad. Shop when you know you're capable of staying focused, and your willpower is stronger, which will help you stick to your shopping resolutions and avoid spending unnecessarily.

- Skip the urge to follow fashion trends... at least until you can afford it in your budget. Fashion trends don't last forever. They come, they go, and the trends can change at the drop of a hat. If you keep chasing the latest fashion trends, you'll find that your savings efforts will be nothing but futile. True, there are on-trend fashion pieces that you can source for cheaper, but that is still money that could have been tucked away into one of the *more important* savings or funding accounts.

- Dryer sheets are one expense that you could save money on by cutting these sheets in half. You stretch the use of the sheets longer, and you still get the same effect you would if you were to use a full sheet.

- Spend a little time doing research and comparing the item you want to buy in other stores. You may find a store or two that is selling it for slightly cheaper, even if it is by a couple of bucks.

- The best way to save as much money as possible on clothing is to eliminate the need to buy clothing frequently. To do that, you need to take good care of the clothes that you have now, especially your favorite items. Basic sewing skills are easy enough to master and will save you hundreds of dollars in the long run, as well as keep you from throwing out items of clothing that are still in good condition.

- If you have to choose, always choose quality over quantity. It may be tempting and more satisfying to see several items in your basket, but fewer pieces that last you longer will save you more money than cheaper pieces that only last a couple of wears.

- Don't throw away your old clothing, use it around the house instead, especially if they have a few more wears left in them before they completely give out. Comfy t-shirts are great for sleeping in, and you don't have to spend the extra dime on a set of pajamas.

- When you have to shop, shop at outlets which offer a return policy, that way if you feel an inkling of regret later on, you can always return the item and get your money back.

Chapter 8:
Saving, Analyzing, Planning

Maybe you haven't been that great with money before, and all you could see happening to your income was money going in and money going straight back out. Your savings wouldn't increase; your debts weren't budging; at times, you wondered why you worked so hard only to have nothing to show for it after several years. The struggle of living paycheck to paycheck *is* absolutely something you can relate to. Now that you know what you need to do with regards to setting a budget, the next stage of the process is how to save, analyze, plan, and track your expenses, so you don't slip back to square one all over again. No matter how deep a financial hole you feel like you've got yourself into, *it is possible* to get out again if you're diligent about it.

The good news is that you now realize something needs to be done, and you're already halfway through doing something about it. You've realized your finances are in trouble, and now you're trying to fix it. *Spend less money than you make.* That is the *only* winning formula that you need to get you to whichever financial goal you've set for yourself. Regardless of your income, the rule is always to spend less than what you make; otherwise, you're in debt. As easy as this sounds, most people end up spending more than they make. Whether you like it or not, and no matter what your spending power is, never go beyond it. Those with a higher salary can afford to go over the budget, but even then, if you don't keep track and manage your finances well, you'd still end up in significant debt or worse, bankruptcy.

The challenge is that no matter how much money you make, your bank account will always have a different agenda, and there always seems to be a way for that money to slip through your fingers. That is *unless* you take control and start keeping track of all your transactions, going both *in* and *out*. Having money be such a taboo topic makes it even more of a challenge to try and succeed in this process yourself. You can't talk about money with family members, friends, or colleagues without the possibility of people feeling judged or downright offended.

Scaling Back Seriously for the Future

After you have tackled simplifying your monthly expenses with the help of your values, priorities, and financial goals, it's now time to work on simplifying your accounts and credit cards. How many credit cards do you currently own? One? Two? Four perhaps? What about a savings account? How many accounts do you own? A simple budget might look towards having just one savings account and only one checking account, and perhaps one credit card for any possible emergencies where you might need one. Everything needs to be removed. The aim is to keep your finances extremely simple, which makes saving money much more comfortable, and makes it simpler to organize your budget when your finances aren't spread out all over the place. Take a good look back at all your past spending habits and purchases, which will then allow you to question any future purchases you're going to make from this point forward. It's important to do an honest evaluation and assessment of just what your spending was so you can determine a pattern or spending habit. Getting to know your spending habits better will lead you to identify when you might be lapsing back into your old ways. It's just as important to rethink all your future purchases by asking the question you already know is coming: *Do I need this?*

Remember, it took you a long time to earn the money that you are now thinking about spending, so every purchase you make needs to *count* and be worth the time and effort spent earning those dollars. There will be changes in your life along the way, which means there's never going to be a perfect plan or budget that you create just the once, and you're then set for life. A constant and regular review of your budget is essential to keeping up with your finances, making sure that this budget *continues* to work for you. Regular reviews also allow you to make any changes or necessary tweaks to your budget to make it work that little bit better. Reviews also give you a chance to observe how well you have managed to stick to what you committed to, and how much progress you've made. Getting organized, simplifying your finances, and setting a successful budget is one thing, but maintaining and implementing it effectively over time is another.

Revamping Your Habits

This is a big change you're about to embark on. Taking control of your finances is by no means going to be easy, especially in the early stages of the process. It's going to require a deep, thoughtful reflection of your current lifestyle and money habits. What is it about your current lifestyle that warrants such change? What about your current lifestyle is unsatisfactory right now? What is your personal reason for wanting to change and plan for your financial future, and is your current lifestyle putting you at a disadvantage? Giving your current situation some deep thought and reflection will help you pinpoint exactly what it is you hope to improve. It will help you be clear about what you want to achieve by putting yourself on the budget pathway.

This is going to be a challenging process, and you need to prepare yourself mentally and emotionally. It *is* going to be uncomfortable, and for some, it may even be a sad process, in having to give up a lot of little luxuries and treats for the greater good. Change rarely ever comes easy, and you are going to have to prepare yourself both mentally and emotionally for this stage of the process. Always think back to how this process is wholly for your benefit; there truly is so much to be gained from this journey. Preparing yourself psychologically, is an integral part of the goal-setting process because if you are not ready in this aspect, it's going to be extremely difficult for you to stick to any goals that you make even if they are small ones.

Budgeting is a habit that must become ingrained as part of your lifestyle. It needs to be so seamlessly integrated into your life as a habit that you don't even think twice about doing it anymore (sort of like eating, taking a shower, brushing your teeth, and washing your face before you go to bed at night). We don't think about those habits. We just do them because they are part of our regular routine. That's the level you want to aim for as you set out to revamp your spending habits right now. It takes about 21 days for something to become a habit, and for that time window, you need to put your full and total effort into adopting this new budget-savvy way of living.

These first 21 days are going to test you to your limits. You're going to encounter all sorts of temptations along the way. You'll want to give up several times, but you know that you shouldn't. You are going to have to be *extremely* disciplined because essentially you are creating a new life and a new habit. You're going to have to put in a lot of effort in these early stages to keep going until it becomes effortless. Make it a point to stick to the new habits you plan to adopt for at least 21 days without fail and watch as it becomes easier from that point on.

Revamping your financial habits is going to boil down to consistency. That is the only way all your planning, analyzing, reviewing, budgeting, and all this hard work you're about to put in is going to pay off. If you want something to become a habit, you must do it on a consistent basis. On your new budget lifestyle journey, you are going to have to make it a matter of daily routine, not something that is done a few times a week because that makes it much harder for it to form into a habit. The more effort that you put into making this a routine, the easier it will be for it to become a habit. The first 21 days are the most crucial part of the process, so don't skip out on even a single day.

Finally, all good budgets and saving strategies need to come with an element of adaptability and flexibility. You may have thought out and planned things down to the smallest detail, and that is great. But if there's one thing we know in life, it's that anything can happen, and things may not always go according to plan. When you set goals for yourself, don't be too rigid with them, and leave some wiggle room for changes and adjustments to be made if necessary. Sometimes, maybe the goal that you have set for the day could be too difficult or taxing because you have had a very stressful and busy day. That's okay, adjust the goal as needed, and make the changes along the way. This makes it much easier for you to stick to your budget. To deal with the unplanned and unexpected, you need to become a person who is willing to adapt and change when the situation calls for it. Otherwise, you're going to find it all too easy to become demotivated and lose momentum each time you're hit with a financial episode that you did not account for.

Tracking Your Income and Expenses for Greater Savings

Money. So easy to spend and so hard to save. You've dreamt about what life would be like if money were no object. Those dreams that live inside everyone who longs for the kind of freedom that only having a strong financial foundation can offer. We've all had those dreams at some point. Now, think about how much you would need to live out those fantasies for real. That's why you've decided to start budgeting and tracking your expenses, right? Because you *want* to now live that kind of life where you no longer have to worry about money. A budget alone is not going to do you any good if you don't regularly review your income and expenses. Once you have figured out what you can live with and without and what kind of income you need to sustain your current lifestyle, it's time to put things in perspective.

Money is going to be the key to a free life, but only if you start doing something about it right now. In order to make your financial future better than what it is today, there's only one thing that needs to happen. You need to start working hard to make it a reality. You don't need to be a financial whiz, a real estate savant, or a savings expert to begin working on developing a smart strategy to start investing in your savings to create wealth. The only requirement you're going to need to bring to the table is your commitment and a strong desire to make it happen. Of course, you need to be sticking to your budget too, that goes without saying.

The best way to know if you are on the right track is to monitor your progress. You must keep an eye on how well you do with adjusting and keeping up with changes and meeting the goals you have set out for yourself. Tracking your progress also makes you responsible and accountable for how well you are doing, and you have something that reminds you of just how well you are doing. When you have a strong desire to succeed, it becomes much easier for you to stick to that commitment. When you keep track of your progress each day, it makes it easier for you to spot which areas may need some improvement. By writing down your progress, you are more likely to follow through than by merely going with the flow. To make sure that your budget is always working for you, this is what you need to do:

- **Limit Your Expense Accounts** - Limit your expenses to just one or two accounts. It is hard to stay on top of your money if money keeps going out of a whole bunch of different accounts. Limit your expenses to *no more than two accounts,* and these should be an account for your bills and an account for your spending. With a billing account, all your bills will be paid through this one account only. Your spending account will allow you to swipe your debit card and make purchases at different stores or grocery stores for the supplies that you need every month. That way, when you're tracking your expenses and reviewing your budget for the month, you're only looking at *two* accounts, and that's it. The whole point is to streamline the process, so it makes your financial planning much easier to analyze at the end of every month. Looking at a whole bunch of different accounts is only going to confuse you and make the entire process more complicated than it needs to be. Remember, if something is too complicated to upkeep, chances are you're not going to be very motivated to stick to it.

- **Track and Review Based On Your Spending Style -** If you spend money more often, then you need to stay on top of your expenses more often. Instead of waiting until the end of the week, try tracking your expenses and filling out your budget spreadsheet every single day. Of course, this can be done once every two days too if you wanted, it really depends on how much you're spending. Take 10-15-minutes out of your day to sit down and look at all your expenses. You want to make sure you're staying on top of things, and even if you kept all the receipts for your transactions, it is still possible to forget one or two expenses along the way if you leave it all for the end of the month or week. If you make it a habit to do this every day, budgeting won't seem like such a chore anymore because you're so used to the process already.

- **Limit Your Expenses Categories and Add Percentages -** If you limit your expenses to just eight or ten categories, it makes it much more straightforward to focus on what is going in and out. In Chapter 4 you can find an example of a budget with 15 categories. Choose your eight or ten categories which reflect your lifestyle and your expenses. During your reviews, this makes it much easier to see if you're spending way too much money in one category and what you can do to cut back. Having these limited categories makes it easier for you to see percentage-wise if you're exceeding the 50/20/30 rule. Once you're looking and evaluating your expenses in set categories and you have percentages next to everything, it will give you an honest overview of exactly where your money is going and if it is going to the right places. This method is going to show you the light and force you to be accountable for your spending habits, which will hopefully give you the motivational boost you need to be more disciplined.

- **A Tracking System On the Go -** Make your budget planning and analysis a lot easier by having some kind of tracking system on the go. *In addition* to your primary budget-tracking method, you should find a way to stay on top of your money on the go. The cash envelope system, for example, is a great way to stay on top of spending cash and if you're doing direct debit transactions, make a note of it in a Notepad app on your devices. You now have the information you need to fill into your main budget spreadsheet at the end of the day. Alternatively, you could turn to one of the many budget tracking apps out there to help you keep tabs while you're on the go if those are something you prefer to manually taking notes. Please remember to download a Simple Budget spreadsheet attached to this book.

Finally, don't forget to congratulate yourself for all your hard work. This was not easy, and you should be proud of every accomplishment you make along the way. Make the reward something which gives you positive reinforcement and makes you feel good about yourself. It also helps to have a little something to look forward to at the end of each week, and it makes the weeks go by much faster - meaning you would reach your 21-day hurdle without even realizing it. This is the best way to feel good and stay motivated to keep going, reward yourself when you have done a fantastic job of sticking to the goals and the habits that you have set yourself for the week. The reward doesn't even have to be anything elaborate. Something as simple as rewarding yourself with your favorite meal, or putting a checkmark next to the accomplishment at the end of each goal can also be a satisfying form of reward.

You Don't Need a Lot of Money to Plan for Your Future

You don't need a lot of money to start planning for your financial future. That is a common misconception. What you need is day-to-day financial management. That's right; your budget is all you need to start. A budget is *the most basic* step you can take to managing your money. Setting savings goals is the next step, and finally, predicting how much income you need to reach those goals. Assuming your future here means retirement, you need to use your budget to plan how much much money it is going to take for you to maintain the lifestyle that you want (how much you're spending) and then multiply that number by 20.

However, at the end of the day, all you can do is plan and prepare. Things change, situations, and circumstances change, and it comes down to the more money you have saved, the better your chances will be of living comfortably in your retirement days. There is no 'magic number' that is going to set you up for a life where you never have to worry again. All you can do is plan to the best of your ability and be disciplined in following a budget.

Chapter 9: Enjoying Your Financial Journey

You're nearly there! You've made it this far already, and you should be incredibly proud of having decided to take control of your finances. You're doing what so few people have managed to accomplish, and this is a fantastic step in the right direction. Financial independence all begins with the right kind of mindset. If you tell yourself from the very start of this journey, *"I CAN DO THIS,"* and you write out that goal visually in front of you, there's no doubt that you *can,* and you *will* be successful in your budgeting efforts.

Saying Goodbye to the Budgeting Lies

Getting your finances healthy and strong again is pretty much the same approach you would take if you were trying to lose weight and start a new healthy lifestyle regime. You need to get rid of unhealthy habits slowly and gradually, phasing them out of your life in stages. It works the same way when you're about to clean up your finances. You need to phase out the unhealthy habits and lies that you sometimes feed yourself in order to feel better about spending money. When you're creating a budget, no matter the amount you're dealing with, you *must be transparent* with yourself about what you realistically spend and what you can realistically afford. It's a mistake that many new first-time budgeters tend to make. Many new budgeters like yourself have a tendency to be overly ambitious, and as a result, they're not honest or realistic about their spending habits.

You need to phase out the 'new budgeting lies' that many first-timers tell themselves in order to give yourself the *best chance* of sticking to your new budget regimen:

- **I'm Not Someone Who Can Keep A Budget -** This is by far *the biggest lie* that people will tell themselves. It is the perfect excuse to *not even bother* creating a budget and staying just where they are: in denial of their spending and wondering why it's so hard to hold onto money. Deciding that you're one of those people who happen to be *'bad with money'* is going to guarantee that you always remain financially illiterate. This is a much easier approach than having to sit down and confront your spending habits. Plus, they love spending too much. They forget, however, that a budget doesn't mean you have to forgo the good stuff. It simply means you need to wait a little longer to get it because you're going to be saving up for it instead of charging it to your credit card. The whole idea of living well for less all boils down to planning. When you plan for anything, you can have your cake and eat it too. If you know that you want something that's going to cost slightly more than you can afford to pay right away, save up for it and wait until you've got the cash to do so.

- **I Don't Mind Drastically Cutting Back On [Name of Category] -** For this example, we'll use the *Eating Out/Going Out* as the category in question. You tell yourself that you don't mind drastically, cutting back on your eating out or going out expenses. This is a typical mistake made by many who attempt to budget for the very first time. In a big, bold move to save more money, they tend to drastically cut back on how much they spend going out or eating out in a month. This includes everything from going out to restaurants, bars, and movies with your friends, significant other, or family. They look at their budget and think, *"Oh, going out is a waste of money. I should cut back on that as much as possible"*. While it is good to want to get rid of non-essential spending right away, you know how crash diets never work out? Well, neither does crash-cutting your spending. What you should be doing instead is looking at exactly how much you spend in your high-expenses categories and then gradually begin *cutting 20%* off that spending and doing so gradually. By slowly cutting back 20% little by little with each budget, it feels less like a struggle as you're being eased into the process. It doesn't make you feel completely deprived either, which is the key to making your budget feel like it's something you can stick to. It gives your brain time to adjust to the budget as the 'new normal.'

- **It's Okay to Have Multiple Credit Cards If I Know How to Control Them -** Nope, this is another lie and a lie that is dangerous too. As long as the credit cards are there, the temptation to spend will never truly go away. Owning one credit card is bad enough, but collecting multiple cards is just a debt disaster waiting to happen. The rewards are never worth the debt you have to pay, no matter what the banks may tell you. When you have to charge even the smallest of unexpected expenses on a credit card, you're on track towards a downward financial spiral. The only way to avoid accumulating debt and unnecessary spending again is to get rid of the credit cards. If you must, only hold on to one for an emergency, but you need to be diligent with it and strict as to what classifies 'an emergency.'

- **I Don't Need to Change My Habits If I Can Control Myself -** You may have successfully paid off some debt in the past, only to find yourself once again in new kinds of debt. Why? Because your spending habits haven't changed. Bad habits need to go if you don't want debt to become a permanent fixture in your life. You're still stuck in that whole *"One day I will"* mentality. One day I will start exercising. One day I will start eating healthy. One day I will start saving some money. Several years later, that 'one day' is still nowhere in sight. The longer you postpone it, the less likely you are to get things done. Habits need to change; it needs to be done now. Not tomorrow, not next week, but *now*, or the 'one-day' mentality is going to hold you back forever.

- **I'm Not Going to Spend Anymore Money In XXX Category -** Another little lie is when you tell yourself you don't need to spend any more money in the XXX category because you don't need it. That is... until you need it. When many budgeters are looking to overhaul their budget or start one for the first time, they start by cutting out a spending category completely, believing that they don't need it, and they can survive just fine without it. The truth is that it's difficult to predict what you will and won't need, and attempting to go cold-turkey right away is the reason why you're going to fall off the budget bandwagon. You're only human, and you will be subject to the occasional need, want, or whim every now and again.

- **It's Okay to Subscribe to Stuff. It's Cheap Enough -** Apple Music, Amazon Prime, Spotify, Netflix, HBO, and more have made it tempting to simply click and subscribe without thinking about the dollars and cents that go with it. It's a subscription world that we're living in. The beauty of technology is that it has made a lot of things so simple and instantaneous. Even our favorite movies and television shows are now available on-demand to watch. As you subscribe to more services, the amount you need to pay each month just to upkeep these subscriptions will quickly increase. Subscribe to far too many things, and you'll find a significant chunk of your payment has to go towards making these payments. How many subscriptions do you really need anyway? If you're not using some of them all that often, it might be time to consider getting rid of them.

- **This Is Going to Be My Only Budget For The Rest Of The Year!** - Oh yes, this is counted as a lie because a budget is not meant to be exactly the same throughout the entire year. Your income and expenses *are* going to fluctuate and change as the year progresses, and you need to be making those little tweaks and adjustments in your budget to reflect these changes. Your budget is an accurate representation of your spending and what goes in and out of your accounts. It's not possible to stick to precisely the same budget throughout the year as nothing remains exactly the same. So many things can happen in a year. Maybe you get a raise at work. You found a side hustle. You had a major expense pop up that you weren't anticipating. A healthy budget means that even if you're earning more, you're not *spending* more because the budget is keeping you in check. Letting a budget sit unchanged for an entire year is guaranteeing that you're not getting the most out of it.

- **I Like Living In the Moment So I Can Learn to Live With Debt If I Have To** - You've come to accept the fact and 'believe' that this is what your life is. Going to work, getting enough of a salary each month to survive, pay your bills, and repeat. You're not earning enough to live in the moment, but you do it anyway because "we only live once." That's how those who live by this mentality find themselves: continually living beyond their means by giving into their impulses whenever they strike. Debt has become such a permanent fixture that you're now not used to saving money as you've been putting it off for so long. This is a dangerous way of thinking that's going to make it hard for you to change your ways. You need to get out of this comfort zone and put all your willpower into breaking this bad habit. You're not 'stuck' in this cycle, you're in it because you choose to be.

- **I've Made A Budget Now I'm All Set and Ready To Get Started -** This little lie is specifically for those who are beginning a new budget for the very first time. While there's no doubt it's fantastic how motivated and full of enthusiasm you are, realistically, since this is your first budget, it is *not* going to be as smooth sailing as you hoped. In fact, it might even be terrible, and that's something you have to be prepared for. Writing out all the numbers and getting it organized is only the first part of the process. A budget is a learning process where you always have to adjust, so just because you've set a budget in place, it doesn't mean everything is going to go perfectly that very first month or that you're not bound to make mistakes along the way. Having a budget for the first time is going to make you hyper-aware of your spending, but the truth is that you're never going to be able to plan your spending down to the finest detail. You need to learn as you go, and that is the best way to handle this process.

The road to financial freedom is a long road, right to the very end. Like the story of the tortoise and the hare, it's important to pace yourself and go slow. Pace yourself in the beginning; this is going to take a little practice before getting comfortable. Diving in headfirst and going about drastically slashing your expenses is only going to shock to your system and lend to the feeling of being deprived. Embrace this new approach in stages if it makes it easier for you to adjust gradually. If you feel resentful and unhappy even from the beginning, you're not going to last very long. Instead of cutting down your expenses by 50% right away, start with 5%, and once you're comfortable, take it up to 10%. Then 15%, 20%, 25% and all the way up to 50%. Go at a pace that suits you.

Easy Money Mistakes to Avoid

Building a financial base that is so solid that not even an unexpected emergency could shake it is going to be well worth all this hard work. One day down the road, you're going to look back and be glad that you made the choice to start when you did. It's during your retirement years that you will really begin to enjoy your financial journey, but that can only happen if you have a strong base to stand on.

- **Not Recording Your Success -** It's easy to feel demotivated when you have no idea how far you've come or how well you're doing. You're doing a good job of tracking your expenses so far, but there's something else you forget to track: *Your little victories along the way.* Not making a list of your victories and little accomplishments is an easy money mistake that gets made by many. Lists don't have to be confined towards just your grocery shopping and debt alone. Keeping tabs on the financial goals, you have successfully accomplished is just as important. The motivation and the thrill that you get when you look back on your past accomplishments, paying off and canceling multiple credit cards, seeing your bank balance growing and flourishing because of your efforts - *that* keeps you going. Those little victories are now going to replace the high you used to get from your former spending sprees since every victory means you're a step closer towards financial freedom.

- **Not Asking, "What's Coming Up?" -** You've planned for the month, and you've organized your sinking fund for those annual or half-yearly big-ticket expenses that you know are coming up. But what about those expenses that are coming up not too long from now? Maybe two or three months from now? For example, if you're a student, you probably know on some level that you've got your textbook expense coming up in another three months, and you'll probably need some new college supplies to go along with it. But have you accounted for this in your budget? That's one mistake that a lot of first time budgeters are guilty of too. You need to be prepared for any expense that is coming, so you never have to dip into your savings fund to do it.

- **Being Impatient and Making Emotional Decisions -** Decisions made solely based on emotions can bring disastrous results. This is true both in life and in budgeting, especially when you are basing them on biased emotions. As eager as you are to see money in the bank and your hard work finally paying off, one of the biggest mistakes you could make is to be too impatient. An unreasonable timeline is what gets the best of most newbie budgeters.

- **Not Designating Specific Intentions -** When you don't set specific targets and intentions for your spending, it can be easy to feel like your finances are the ones running the show while you watch helplessly from the sidelines. It can be incredibly frustrating to feel like you're failing *even* when you're on a budget, but if this is happening, then it could be from a lack of intention with your budget.

- **Not Being Flexible Enough** - Your budget needs to be flexible, and so does your mindset. If you're always going to feel stressed whenever something unexpected happens, or your financial plans don't go the way you want them to, you'll be continually overwhelmed by your finances. That's what a regular budget review is for. To give you an opportunity to assess if you're staying on the right track despite the unexpected. Be flexible and be willing to adapt and change, or it's going to be tough to stick to any kind of budget if you're mentally and subconsciously rigid and resistant.

You'll Enjoy the Fruits of Your Labor Soon Enough

In any kind of challenging process, it never hurts to have all the support that you need. Your first line of support is going to be your family, of course. You're entirely reinventing your finances as you know it, and it's going to help you if your family understands this and gets on board with it. Couples and families need to talk about important financial decisions being made, and choosing to now live frugally is an important decision. Use family discussion time to try and work towards building some common financial goals that everyone can pitch in and work together on. Having that familial support is essential in encouraging each other to keep going during the times that it hits you the hardest.

Yes, it is going to be hard in the beginning, but hard work never hurts anybody. Especially when you know that a reward is waiting for you at the end. That reward is none other than financial freedom and a debt-free life. A budget doesn't have to feel like a prison sentence. Adopt a positive mindset and remind yourself this is for a very good reason. Your budget should be made in a way that works for you. You don't have to say "no" to every single thing when you choose to put yourself on a budget. You're just more selective with your purchases than you were before. Everything that you buy from now on is going to be based on your budget and your priorities. When you want to indulge occasionally, and you've got the funds to spare, go ahead and do it. You need that kind of balance in your life to keep you feeling happy and motivated.

Conclusion

Think it's too late to start taking control? *Think again.* **It's *never* too late to start.** The only thing that is going to be stopping you from making progress with your finances is *you*. Your age has nothing to do with it, because it's never too late, especially not with how quickly things change. Think of what your life could be like without stressing over money. To never have to count the days until the next paycheck once again. A life where you're never scraping the bottom of the barrel because you have everything that you need to survive comfortably.

Imagine being so *in control* of your finances that the days until the next time you get paid will come and go so quickly you'll hardly notice. Think age is a problem? *Think again.* Anyone can start creating a budget for themselves that is going to change everything. You're only as 'old' as you allow yourself to think that you are. Sure, you may not be in your 20s anymore or just starting out in your first job. You could be in your late 30s or maybe even 40s when you're reading this, but even then, *it is not too late.* Instead of using age as a barrier that stops you from living your best life, embrace your age because it comes with wisdom. You may not be in your 20s, but see this as a good thing, it just means all your life experience can now be put to good use for your advantage.

Thinking it's too late to start is nothing more than an excuse. The longer you hold onto it, the more it is going to hold *you* back in life. Your finances are the way to personal freedom and saying goodbye to debt once and for all. Even when you're on a budget, there is absolutely no reason why you can't still be happy and make time for the things you love to enjoy. It all comes down to how well you manage your money and shift it around. After a while, you'll get better and wiser with your finances, and when you begin to find that balance between not overspending but still being happy with the lifestyle you lead, a budget is going to be the best thing you ever made for yourself.

Whenever you encounter a bump in the road or a setback that threatens to derail your motivation, reflect on Benjamin Franklin's wise words again: *If you fail to plan, then you will plan to fail.* It is always better to have a plan for your finances than to have no plan at all. Setbacks will happen, sometimes you'll take a step back or two, but the beauty of using a budget as a guide is that you can *always* bounce back.

Set your financial plan, use all the resources, advice, tips, and strategies you've encountered in the chapters of this book, and let this be the roadmap that points you in the right direction. Be willing to be flexible and adaptable, regularly review your budget, make adjustments as necessary, and, most of all, have your goals at the forefront of your mind to lead the way. Making more money is not the answer. Staying *in control* of your money is the key to making a difference. Stay committed, stick to it, and I promise you this is absolutely going to be *worth it!*

Resources

6 Reasons Why You Need a Budget. (n.d.). Retrieved from https://www.investopedia.com/financial-edge/1109/6-reasons-why-you-need-a-budget.aspx

6-Step Guide to Creating a Monthly Household Budget. (n.d.). Retrieved from https://www.thebalance.com/creating-a-household-budget-960839

7 Reasons Why You Should Budget Your Money. (n.d.). Retrieved from https://www.thebalance.com/reasons-to-budget-money-2385699

7 tips on how to budget and save. (n.d.). Retrieved from https://www.heritage.com.au/help-and-guidance/saving-and-budgeting/7-steps-to-review-your-budget

10 Personal Saving Tips. (n.d.). Retrieved from https://www.workingmother.com/money-talks/10-personal-saving-tips#page-9

10 Budgeting Mistakes You Need to Stop Making. (n.d.). Retrieved from https://www.thebalance.com/biggest-budgeting-mistakes-2385610

B. (2016, October 28). 9 Reasons Why You Should Track Expenses. Retrieved from https://www.invoiceberry.com/blog/9-reasons-track-expenses/

Bell, M. (2019, August 16). Why You Should Review Your Budget Often. Retrieved from https://www.crosswalk.com/family/finances/budget/why-you-should-review-your-budget-often.html

Bieber, C. (2018, June 4). Budgeting 101: How to Start Budgeting for the First Time. Retrieved from https://www.fool.com/investing/2018/04/21/budgeting-101-how-to-start-budgeting-for-the-first.aspx

Buchenau, Z. (2020, January 27). 10 Reasons You Should Track Your Expenses. Retrieved from https://bethebudget.com/reasons-to-track-your-expenses/

Buchenau, Z. (2020b, February 14). How Often Should You Review Your Budget? Retrieved from https://bethebudget.com/how-often-should-you-review-your-budget/#:%7E:text=Reviewing%20your%20budget%20helps%20you,key%20element%20of%20personal%20finance.

Carter, S. M. (2018, March 20). 30% of Americans are "constantly" stressed out about money—but you don't have to be. Retrieved from https://www.cnbc.com/2018/03/19/30-percent-of-americans-are-stressed-out-about-money-constantly.html

Dawson, E. (2018, November 25). 6 Common Budget Mistakes That Are Costing You More Than You Realize. Retrieved from https://medium.com/datadriveninvestor/6-common-budget-mistakes-that-are-costing-you-more-than-you-realize-9a7310197d0b

Expert, C. (2020, January 17). Sinking Funds Explained - Queensland - SSKB - Strata Managers | Community Experts. Retrieved from https://sskb.com.au/sinking-funds-explained-queensland/#:%7E:text=A%20body%20corporate's%20sinking%20fund,%2C%20or%20non%2Drecurrent%20items.

Falk, T. (2020, April 27). What's a sinking fund and how do they work? Retrieved from https://www.finder.com.au/sinking-funds

Financial Advice Married Couples Should Not Ignore. (n.d.). Retrieved from https://www.thebalance.com/financial-advice-for-married-couples-2302874

Finn, C. (2018, August 31). 6 Simple Ways to Finally Organize Receipts. Retrieved from https://thediyplaybook.com/6-ways-to-organize-receipts/

Habits, B. M. (2018, September 17). 5 Ways to Stick to Your Budget. Retrieved from https://bettermoneyhabits.bankofamerica.com/en/saving-budgeting/how-to-stick-to-a-budget

Hannum, C. (2017, November 16). How To Get Out Of Debt (And 7 Reasons You're Still In It). Retrieved from https://www.self.com/story/7-reasons-youre-still-in-debt-and-how-to-finally-break-the-cycle

Hogan, C. (2020, June 17). Can You Retire on $1 Million? Retrieved from https://www.daveramsey.com/blog/can-you-retire-on-1-million

How Income Volatility Interacts With American Families' Financial Security. (2017, March 9). Retrieved from https://www.pewtrusts.org/en/research-and-analysis/issue-briefs/2017/03/how-income-volatility-interacts-with-american-families-financial-security

How Maslow's Famous Hierarchy of Needs Explains Human Motivation. (n.d.). Retrieved from https://www.verywellmind.com/what-is-maslows-hierarchy-of-needs-4136760

How to Create a Family Budget (Easy Step-By-Step Budgeting). (2019, November 12). Retrieved from https://www.mint.com/budgeting-3/how-to-create-a-budget-step-by-step

How to Stick to Your Budget. (n.d.). Retrieved from https://www.everydollar.com/blog/steps-to-help-you-stick-to-your-budget

Johnston, J. (2020, May 22). 10 Ways to Save Money on Monthly Rent Payments. Retrieved from https://www.incharge.org/financial-literacy/budgeting-saving/how-to-save-money-on-rent/

Joy, D. (2019, October 15). How To Set Financial Goals: 6 Simple Steps. Retrieved from https://www.incharge.org/financial-literacy/budgeting-saving/how-to-set-financial-goals/

Klaw, M. (2019, November 5). My Husband Controls The Money. Retrieved from https://www.hermoney.com/connect/marriage/marriage-mistakes-women-make/

Learn How to Evaluate Your Budget to Help You Reach Your Goals Faster. (n.d.). Retrieved from https://www.thebalance.com/how-to-evaluate-your-budget-2385694

Learn How to Manage Seasonal Expenses | Personal or Household Budget. (n.d.). Retrieved from https://www.nomoredebts.org/budgeting/budgeting-strategies/seasonal-expenses-save-money

lifehackerinternational. (2019, May 9). How To Save Money On Groceries. Retrieved from https://www.lifehacker.com.au/2019/05/how-to-save-money-on-groceries/

Lisa, A. (2020, May 7). 20 Worst Money Mistakes People Make in the Name of Love. Retrieved from https://www.gobankingrates.com/saving-money/relationships/worst-money-mistakes-couples-make/

Managing Your Finances Like A Supermom! (n.d.). Retrieved from https://www.workingmother.com/managing-your-finances-like-supermom

Mcleod, S. (2020, March 20). Maslow's Hierarchy of Needs. Retrieved from https://www.simplypsychology.org/maslow.html#:%7E:text=Maslow's%20hierarchy%20of%20needs%20is,hierarchical%20levels%20within%20a%20pyramid.&text=From%20the%20bottom%20of%20the,esteem%2C%20and%20self%2Dactualization.

Maslow's Hierarchy of Needs Explained. (n.d.). Retrieved from https://www.thoughtco.com/maslows-hierarchy-of-needs-4582571

McLean, R. (2020, January 15). 10 Common Budgeting Mistakes You Might Be Making. Retrieved from https://onproperty.com.au/common-budgeting-mistakes/

MyMoneyCoach - Money Management Basics. (n.d.). Retrieved from https://www.mymoneycoach.ca/money-management/budgeting-plan-for-future

O'Shea, B. (2020, January 16). Budgeting 101: How to Create a Budget. Retrieved from https://www.nerdwallet.com/blog/finance/how-to-build-a-budget/

P. (2020, June 24). 5 Simple Steps to Create a Successful Budget. Retrieved from https://www.payoff.com/life/money/5-simple-steps-to-create-a-successful-budget/

Reviewing your business budget regularly. (2018, September 26). Retrieved from https://www.nibusinessinfo.co.uk/content/reviewing-your-business-budget-regularly

Seasonal Budgeting. (n.d.). Retrieved from https://www.practicalmoneyskills.com/learn/budgeting/seasonal_budgeting

Solutions, R. (2020, May 8). 10 Reasons People Stay in Debt. Retrieved from https://www.daveramsey.com/blog/why-do-people-stay-in-debt

Solutions, R. (2020a, April 24). How to Save Money on Groceries. Retrieved from https://www.daveramsey.com/blog/ways-to-save-on-groceries

Step 1: Set Goals. (n.d.). Retrieved from https://www.mymoneycoach.ca/money-management/set-financial-goals

Step 2: Identify Income and Expenses. (n.d.). Retrieved from https://www.mymoneycoach.ca/money-management/identify-income-expenses

Step 3: Separate Needs from Wants. (n.d.). Retrieved from https://www.mymoneycoach.ca/money-management/separating-needs-from-wants

Step 4: Design Your Budget. (n.d.). Retrieved from https://www.mymoneycoach.ca/money-management/budget-design+

Step 5: Put Your Plan into Action. (n.d.). Retrieved from https://www.mymoneycoach.ca/money-management/implement-financial-plan

Step 6: Manage Seasonal Expenses. (n.d.). Retrieved from https://www.mymoneycoach.ca/money-management/manage-seasonal-expenses

Step 7: Looking Ahead. (n.d.). Retrieved from https://www.mymoneycoach.ca/money-management/financial-planning-future

Tatham, M. (2020, April 16). 2019 Consumer Credit Review. Retrieved from https://www.experian.com/blogs/ask-experian/consumer-credit-review/

What is Budgeting and Why is it Important? (n.d.). Retrieved from https://www.mymoneycoach.ca/budgeting/what-is-a-budget-planning-forecasting

Why Tracking Your Expenses Is Important. (2019, September 30). Retrieved from https://www.positivelendingsolutions.com.au/resource s/information-centre/why-tracking-your-expenses-is-important/#:%7E:text=Expenses%20tracking%20is%2 0essential%20in,achieve%20the%20lifestyle%20you%2 0want.

Your 6-Step Guide to Making a Personal Budget. (n.d.). Retrieved from https://www.thebalance.com/how-to-make-a-budget-1289587

Gerard Hoffman

www.ingramcontent.com/pod-product-compliance
Lightning Source LLC
Chambersburg PA
CBHW071649210326
41597CB00017B/2166